Zombie cupcakes

Zilly Rosen

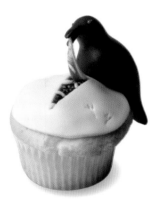

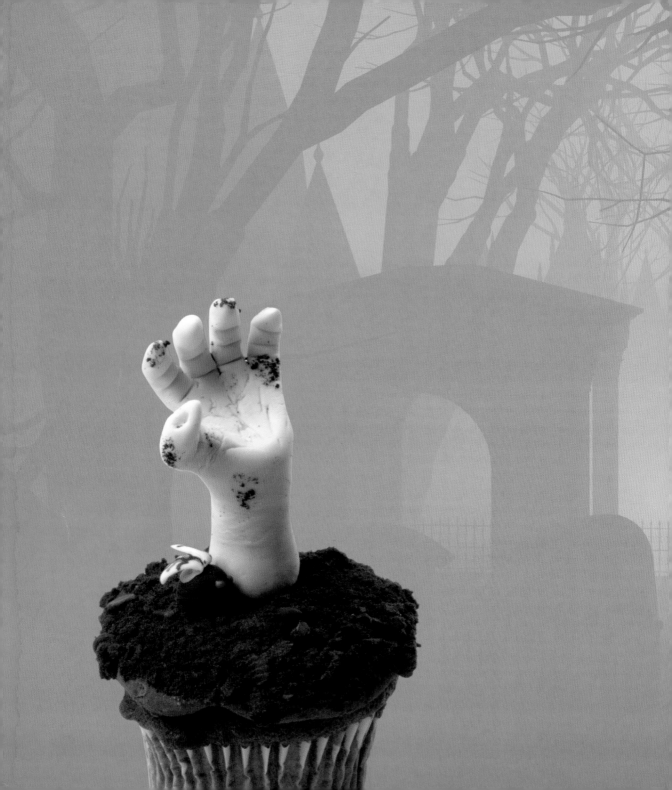

Zombie
cupcakes

Zilly Rosen

Andrews McMeel
Publishing, LLC
Kansas City • Sydney • London

Zombie Cupcakes

Copyright © Ivy Press Limited 2010

ANDREWS McMEEL PUBLISHING, LLC
an Andrews McMeel Universal company
1130 Walnut Street
Kansas City, Missouri 64106
www.andrewsmcmeel.com

ISBN: 978-1-4494-0112-2

This book was conceived, designed, and produced by

Ivy Press
210 High Street
Lewes
East Sussex BN7 2NS
United Kingdom
www.ivy-group.co.uk

Creative Director **Peter Bridgewater**
Publisher **Jason Hook**
Editorial Director **Tom Kitch**
Senior Designer **James Lawrence**
Editors **Susanna Tee** and **Jo Richardson**
Designer **Glyn Bridgewater**
Photographer **Michelle Zurowski**
Illustrator **Sarah Skeate**

The author would like to thank Hannah Russell for all her artistic contributions and tireless labor on the book, and the fearless Shannon Pilarski, whose knowledge of all things zombie is only exceeded by her creativity and her sculpting ability. Without Shannon, the undead decorations in this book would never have come to life.

The publisher would like to thank the following for permission to reproduce copyright material:
Getty Images/Bill Pugliano/Stringer: front cover; Fotolia/AlienCat: 2; Gabrel: 16; Imyme: 16; Dmytro Konstantynov: 20; Andreas Gradin: 24, 26; Alexei Novikov: 28; Steven Smith: 32; Sergey: 36; Ivan Bliznetsov: 38, 44; lassedesignen: 40; fotoandmakeup: 42; Mary Lan: 52; Shutterstock/Cajoer: 3; Fribus Ekaterina: 18; iStockphoto/Joshua Blake: 6.

Printed in China

Color origination by Ivy Press Reprographics

11 12 13 14 15 IYP 12 11 10 9 8 7 6 5 4 3 2 1

Notes for the Reader

Teaspoon measurements are assumed to be 5 ml and tablespoons are assumed to be 15 ml. Milk is assumed to be whole unless otherwise stated.

Pregnant and breastfeeding women are advised to avoid eating peanuts and peanut products. Ready-made ingredients used in the recipes in this book may contain nuts—sufferers from nut allergies should check any ingredients' packaging before use.

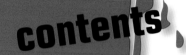

contents

toxic bite

t-virus

biohazard
ingested

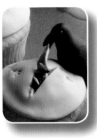
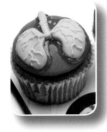
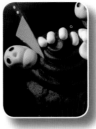
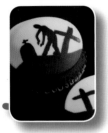
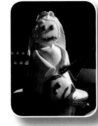
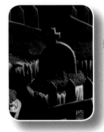
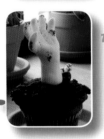
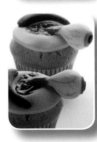
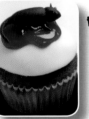
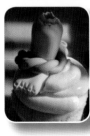
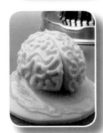
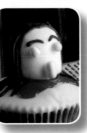
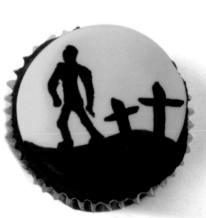

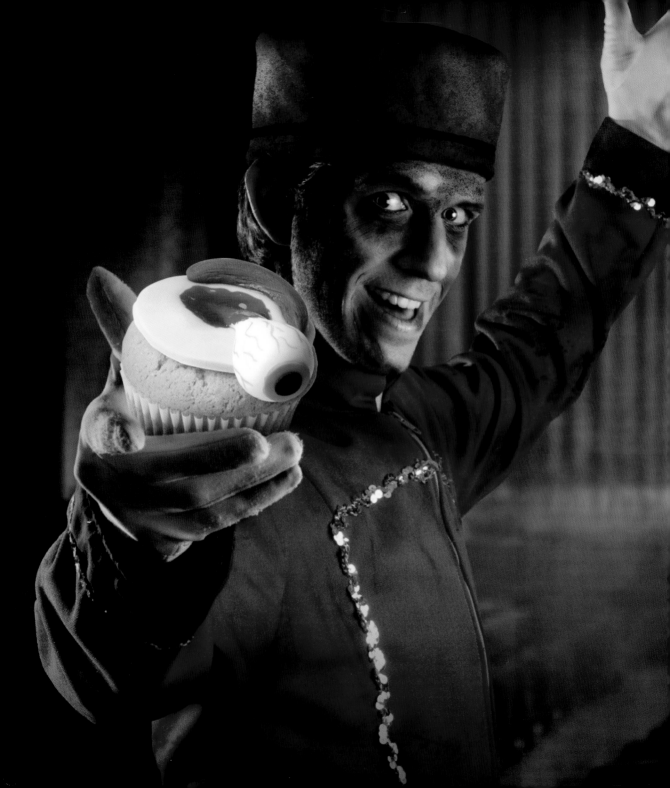

introduction

Zombies are on the march. It is too late to turn them back. Their animated corpses are shambling out of the graveyards and taking over every aspect of popular culture before our very eyes. Vying for world domination with another undead creature, the timeless and seductive vampire, the zombie is resurrecting itself and infecting armies of devoted followers in comics, video games, movies, and television, and even in "mash-ups" of the novels of Jane Austen, who is no doubt turning in her grave. So what are zombies, and why are they now emerging through the cracked frosting of that other irresistible craze, the cupcake?

Well, the flesh-eating undead can be traced back to ancient mythology and to the infamous voodoo traditions of Haiti, but the modern zombie is generally considered to have risen from *Night of the Living Dead*, the horror movie made in 1968 by the legendary director George A. Romero. Here, we encounter the characteristic slow-moving army of plague-infested ghouls that threatens to overwhelm the human race, giving birth to the dead-eyed, rotting creature that now has its own genre. Certainly, the popularity of zombies in books and movies rises and falls, but like the creatures themselves they just keep on coming; and they are currently, without question, on the march. And what better way to celebrate zombies than with another phenomenon that has refused to die off, defying its critics and its nature to become bigger and bigger, and spawning culinary followers from celebrity chefs to café owners around the globe? The cupcake bar might not immediately seem the natural home of the zombie, but who said that these delicious little creations all had to be universally cute? Whether you wish to finally find a party food that does justice to Halloween horror, to bake a bite-size offering that was just made for trick-or-treating, or simply to create fashionable party cupcakes that will have your legions of guests marching on the kitchen to ask for more, the time is undeniably ripe for cupcakes to rise from their graves of cuteness and reveal their dark hearts. Putting the sickly into the sweet taste of these delicious treats, this book offers you a sugar-coated carnage of graveyards, body parts, and rotting monsters that will ensure adults and children alike squeal in delighted horror before sinking their teeth into the frosted flesh and realizing that zombies never tasted so good. Welcome to the graveyard of traditional cupcakes. Enter at your own risk...

Delicious Eye Poppers are the perfect treat to usher in your guests.

basic recipes

The cupcakes in this book use a variety of basic recipes for the decorations and toppings. The quantity of each basic recipe used varies from cupcake to cupcake, so check the cupcake recipe before you start. You may wish to make smaller batches of the basic recipes, or you can store the leftovers for use with other cupcakes. Bear in mind that the basic recipes don't all keep for the same amount of time.

White fondant can easily be bought from specialized cake-decorating stores or suppliers, along with a variety of different colors. However, if you have difficulty buying colored fondant, you can color it yourself. Half & Half (see page 11) can be colored in the same way.

Many decorations need to be cut using a craft knife. Take the same care when using a craft knife to cut the decorations as you would when cutting paper, and make sure you keep it out of the reach of children.

dark chocolate ganache

**Makes enough to
cover 12 to 14 cupcakes**

- 2¾ cups mini semisweet chocolate chips
- 2 cups heavy cream
- 1 tsp unsalted butter

1 Put the chocolate chips in a large heatproof bowl. Bring the cream to a boil in a medium saucepan over high heat.

2 Just before the cream comes to a full boil, pour the cream into the chocolate chips and whisk together until smooth.

3 Add the butter and stir until smooth and shiny. Place plastic wrap directly over the surface to prevent a skin from forming, then let stand at room temperature overnight to cool. Store in the refrigerator, covered, for up to 3 weeks.

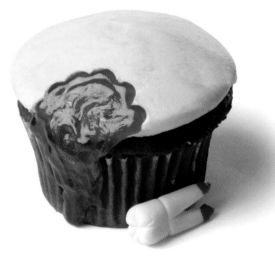

Italian meringue buttercream

Makes enough to cover 12 to 14 cupcakes

- 1 cup plus 2 tbsp granulated sugar
- ¼ cup water
- 6 large egg whites
- 1½ cups (12 oz/3 sticks) unsalted butter, softened, cut into small pieces
- 1 tsp pure vanilla extract
- pinch of salt

flavors

chocolate: 3 oz semisweet chocolate, melted
caramel: 2 tbsp dulce de leche and ⅛ tsp salt
coffee: 1 tbsp instant espresso powder dissolved in 1 tsp boiling water
amaretto: ½ to 1 tsp almond extract
coconut: 1 tsp coconut extract and 1 tbsp coconut milk

1 Put the sugar and water in a large saucepan and stir together. Bring to a rolling boil on high heat, then boil undisturbed for 5 minutes.

2 Allow the sugar mixture to continue boiling while you put the egg whites in the bowl of a large freestanding electric mixer and beat on high until stiff.

3 Continuing to beat on high, carefully hold the pan with the sugar syrup well above the bowl and slowly pour the syrup into the egg whites in a thin stream, without allowing it to touch the beater.

4 Continue to beat the egg white mixture on high for 10 minutes or until cool.

5 With the machine still running, add the pieces of butter and mix until combined.

6 Reduce the speed to low, add the vanilla extract and salt, and continue to mix until combined.

7 To flavor the buttercream, add the ingredients for your chosen flavor at the end of mixing.

8 Store in the refrigerator, covered, for up to 3 weeks or in small amounts in the freezer for up to 3 months. Before use, return to room temperature and then beat until smooth and the texture is restored.

royal icing

Makes about 8 oz

- 1 large egg white, plus extra if necessary
- pinch of cream of tartar
- 1¾ to 2 cups confectioners' sugar, sifted
- paste food coloring (optional)

1 Put the egg white and cream of tartar in the bowl of a large freestanding electric mixer and beat together until frothy.

2 With the machine still running, gradually add the confectioners' sugar until the mixture begins to stiffen and turn opaque white. Scrape down the sides of the bowl and beat briefly on high. The mixture should be stiff but still pliable.

3 If necessary, thin the mixture with a little extra egg white or a drop of food coloring. Cover with a damp dish towel to prevent a crust from forming. To store, put it in a container, place plastic wrap directly over the surface to prevent a skin from forming, and seal the container. Keep in the refrigerator for up to 1 week.

4 To color the icing, add the appropriate paste food coloring in drops or on a toothpick or the tip of a knife and beat in until you achieve the desired color.

cream cheese frosting

Makes enough to cover 12 cupcakes

- 1½ cups (about 12¼ oz) cream cheese, at room temperature
- 4 tbsp (2 oz/½ stick) unsalted butter, softened
- ½ tsp pure vanilla extract
- ¾ cup confectioners' sugar
- pinch of salt
- ¼ tsp lemon juice

1 Put the cream cheese and butter in a large bowl and beat with a wooden spoon until soft and light. Add the vanilla extract and mix together.

2 Sift in the confectioners' sugar and salt, add the lemon juice, and mix together until well combined. Store in the refrigerator, covered, for up to 3 days.

piping gel "blood"

Makes about 3 oz

- 3 oz clear piping gel
- 4 to 5 drops red paste food coloring

1 Put the piping gel in a small bowl, add the paste food coloring in drops or on a toothpick or the tip of a knife, and stir in until you achieve a deep blood red color. Store according to the directions on the gel package.

half & half

Makes about 8 oz

- 4 oz store-bought white fondant
- 4 oz ready-to-use gum paste
- plain vegetable shortening (as needed)

1 Knead the fondant and then the gum paste separately on a counter until smooth, then combine and knead until well mixed. If the mixture becomes sticky, add a little shortening.

2 Cover with an upturned bowl or cup to prevent a crust from forming. To store, roll the mixture into a ball, double wrap in plastic wrap, and keep in a sealed container at room temperature for up to two weeks.

rolling out half & half for cupcake toppers

- acetate sheets (available from art and crafts or cake-decorating stores or suppliers)
- plain vegetable shortening, for sticking and greasing
- Half & Half (see left)

1 Cut a strip of acetate to the size directed by the recipe. Put shortening under the strip to stick it to the counter and grease the strip liberally with more shortening.

2 Place the Half & Half on the acetate and roll out very thinly to a thickness of ⅛ inch or less. Using a craft knife, cut as directed in the recipe. Let dry, uncovered, overnight.

coloring fondant & half & half

- store-bought white fondant or Half & Half (see page left)
- drops of paste food coloring (as directed by the recipe)
- plain vegetable shortening, for greasing

1 Place the fondant in a large bowl. Add as many drops of paste food coloring as directed by the recipe. When instructed to add a dab of coloring, use the end of a toothpick to pick up a very small amount of coloring, then mix it in the fondant or Half & Half.

2 Lightly grease the counter with a little shortening and knead the mixture until evenly colored. If necessary, add a little shortening to the frosting to prevent it from becoming sticky. Add more food coloring as needed until the color is the desired shade.

zombie bits & pieces

Many of the cupcake recipes in this book have extra decorative details. We've included a selection of ideas here, from maggots and flies to improvised weapons for fighting back the zombie hordes. Some recipes suggest the most appropriate decorations for you to use, but obviously you could add them to any of the recipes in the book or to use them to decorate your own zombie cupcake creations.

When you're hosting a party, you could scatter these bits and pieces between the cupcakes if you're presenting the cupcakes as an ensemble, or if you're presenting a larger spread of food, then perhaps dot them around the table on napkins.

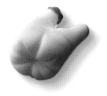

teeth

Makes 12

- 1½ oz plain white Half & Half (see page 11)

1 Roll the Half & Half into 12 oval shapes. Make a cut in the middle of the oval that extends halfway up to create the roots. Pinch the ends of the roots to a point.

2 Use the side of a toothpick to indent 2 crisscrossed lines on the rounded end of the tooth. Use the end of the toothpick to make additional creases and crevices so that the tooth looks like a molar.

3 Press the side of the toothpick all the way around the tooth to make the groove that separates the tooth from the root. Repeat to make another 11 teeth. Let dry overnight. Store, uncovered, in a cool, dry place, but not in the refrigerator.

maggots

Makes 12

- ¼ to ½ oz plain white Half & Half (see page 11)

1 Roll the Half & Half into a ball and then pinch off tiny amounts. Roll between your finger and thumb into small lengths. Let dry overnight. Store, uncovered, in a cool, dry place, but not the refrigerator.

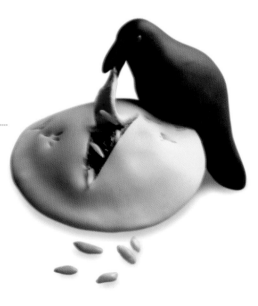

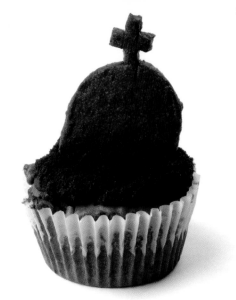

gravestones & crosses

Makes 6 of each

- 1½ tsp instant espresso powder
- ½ tsp boiling water
- 2 cups white all-purpose, cake, or pastry flour, plus extra for dusting
- ½ cup unsweetened cocoa
- pinch of salt
- 1 cup (8 oz/2 sticks) unsalted butter, softened
- 1 cup granulated sugar
- 1 large egg, beaten
- 2 tsp pure vanilla extract
- 1¾ oz plain white Royal Icing, for decorating (see page 10; optional)

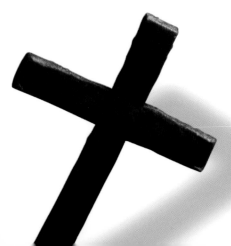

1 Preheat the oven to 325°F. Line a baking sheet with parchment paper. Dissolve the espresso powder in the boiling water. Sift the flour, cocoa, and salt together.

2 Put the butter and sugar in a large bowl and, using an electric mixer, beat together until pale in color. Add the egg, vanilla extract, and espresso liquid and mix together until combined.

3 Add the sifted ingredients to the mixture, in 3 equal batches, and mix until just blended. Wrap the dough in plastic wrap and chill in the refrigerator for about 1 hour.

4 Roll the dough out on a lightly floured counter to a thickness of ⅛ to ¼ inch. Using a sharp knife, cut 2 long strips of dough ½ inch wide, then cut into 6 strips 4½ inches long. From the remaining dough, cut out 6 rectangles 2 by 1½ inches.

5 To make the gravestones, cut the top off each rectangle in a curve. Transfer the rectangles to the prepared baking sheet.

6 To make the crosses, place a strip of dough on the baking sheet. Cut two 1 by ½-inch pieces from another strip of dough. Press the 2 smaller pieces onto either side of the long strip about one-third of the way down. Make sure that the dough is touching so that the parts will bake together and come out as a single shape.

7 Bake in the oven for 10 to 12 minutes, turning the cookies once, until set but not dark on the edges. Let cool for 30 minutes.

8 If desired, fit a pastry bag or a parchment paper cone fitted with a fine plain piping tip and fill with the Royal Icing. Pipe the names of people you know or great zombie movie directors on the gravestones.

rats

Makes 2

- 1 oz Half & Half, colored black with 3 drops black paste food coloring (see page 11)
- 1 oz Royal Icing, colored red with 4 drops red paste food coloring (see page 10)

flies

Makes 12

- 1½ oz Half & Half, colored black with 4 drops black paste food coloring (see page 11)
- 1 oz plain white Half & Half
- 1 oz Royal Icing, colored red with 4 drops red paste food coloring (see page 10)
- red edible marker pen
- black edible marker pen

1 Divide the black Half & Half into 12 small balls and then shape into ovals for the bodies. Divide the white Half & Half into 24 small ovals for the wings. Pinch the ovals flat.

2 Press a wing oval down on the handle of a wooden spoon to curve, angling inward. Press a second wing oval down on the spoon so that it overlaps the first, angling inward from the opposite side. Use a little water to join the wings where they overlap. Repeat to make 11 more pairs of wings. Let set for about 10 minutes.

3 When the wings have set, curve the joined edge under to create a surface to attach to the body. Use a little water to attach the wings to the center of the body.

4 Use a small amount of red Royal Icing in a pastry bag or parchment paper cone fitted with a fine plain piping tip to pipe 2 eyes on the fly. Use the edible marker pens to make lines on the wings. Repeat to make the other 11 flies. Let dry overnight. Store, uncovered, in a cool, dry place, but not in the refrigerator.

1 Roll most of the Half & Half into 2 balls. Pinch one end of a ball into a small point to make the rat's nose. Pull and pinch the other end to make an elongated, thin tail. To make the head appear separate from the body, take the side of a toothpick and roll it around the Half & Half where the neck would be. Repeat to make another rat.

2 To make the ears, roll the remaining Half & Half into 4 tiny balls and squeeze them flat. Use a small amount of water to attach the ears to the rats' heads. Use the toothpick to smooth the area where they join if your fingers seem too big.

3 Fit a pastry bag or a parchment paper cone with a fine plain piping tip and fill with the red Royal Icing. Pipe a beady eye on either side of each head. Let dry overnight. Store, uncovered, in a cool, dry place, but not in the refrigerator.

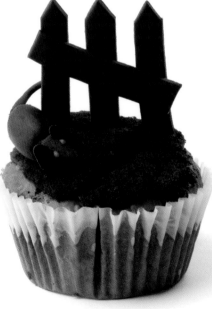

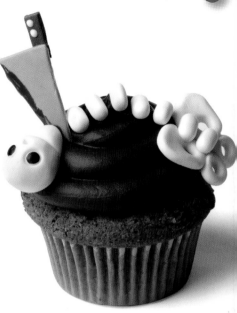

knives

Makes 12

- 2 oz Half & Half, colored gray with 1 drop black paste food coloring (see page 11)
- ½ oz Half & Half, colored brown with 3 drops brown paste food coloring
- 1 oz plain white Royal Icing (see page 10)
- plain vegetable shortening, for greasing

1 Roll out the gray Half & Half very thinly on an acetate strip greased with shortening. Cut 6 rectangles, each measuring ½ by 1 inch. Cut diagonally across each rectangle to create 2 triangular knife blades.

2 Roll out the brown Half & Half very thinly on an acetate strip greased with shortening. Cut into a rectangle measuring ½ by 1 inch. Cut in half lengthwise, then make 5 evenly spaced vertical cuts to make knife handles.

3 Using the white Royal Icing in a pastry bag or parchment paper cone fitted with a fine plain piping tip, attach a knife handle to the corner of each knife blade. Pipe 2 dots on each handle to represent rivets. Let dry overnight. Store, uncovered, in a cool, dry place, but not in the refrigerator.

baseball bats

Makes 4

- 2½ oz Half & Half, colored pale brown with 1 drop brown and 1 drop yellow paste food coloring (see page 11)

1 Roll the Half & Half into 4 thin sausage shapes that are thicker at one end and gradually become thinner at the other end. Cut the thinner end so that it is blunt. Push the blunt end to create the handle of the bat.

2 Use a toothpick, rolled on the edge, to define the handle of the bat further. Repeat to make another 3 bats. Let dry overnight. Store in a cool, dry place, but not in the refrigerator.

crowbars

Makes 4

- 1 oz Half & Half, colored black with 3 drops black paste food coloring (see page 11)

1 Roll the Half & Half into 4 thin sausage shapes. A quarter of the way down, bend the sausage shape at a right angle, then pinch the short end flat.

2 Use a craft knife to cut a "V" out of the flat end of the crowbar. Repeat to make another 3 crowbars. Let dry overnight. Store, uncovered, in a cool, dry place, but not in the refrigerator.

shovels

Makes 4

- 1½ oz Half & Half, colored gray with a dab of black paste food coloring (see page 11)
- 1½ oz Half & Half, colored pale brown with 1 drop brown and 1 drop yellow paste food coloring

1 Roll the gray Half & Half into 4 balls. Squeeze each into a triangle shape. Flatten the triangle to create the blade of the shovel. Pinch the edges so that it appears to be sharp, especially at the point.

2 Roll one quarter of the pale brown Half & Half into a thin sausage shape 3 inches long. Flatten one end and attach it to the back of the shovel blade with water. Repeat to make another 3 shovels. Let dry overnight. Store, uncovered, in a cool, dry place, but not in the refrigerator.

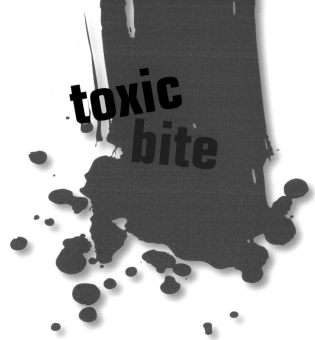

DIFFICULTY RATING

MAKES **12**

Decorations can be made the same day as baking.

red velvet
cupcakes

- ½ cup buttermilk
- ½ tsp pure vanilla extract
- ½ tsp distilled malt vinegar
- 1 tbsp red liquid food coloring
- ½ cup (4 oz/1 stick) unsalted butter, softened
- ¾ cup granulated sugar
- 2 large eggs, beaten
- 1⅓ cups all-purpose, cake, or pastry flour
- 1 tbsp unsweetened cocoa
- ½ tsp baking soda
- ¼ tsp salt

decorations

- 1 drop peach paste food coloring
- 1 quantity Italian Meringue Buttercream (see page 9)
- 4½ oz Piping Gel "Blood" (see page 10)
- 12 Teeth (see page 12)

All it takes is just one bite from a zombie and you will turn into one of the undead. This red velvet cupcake, on the other hand, is so delicious that you won't be able to stop at one bite—instead you will keep on munching until you have devoured the whole thing.

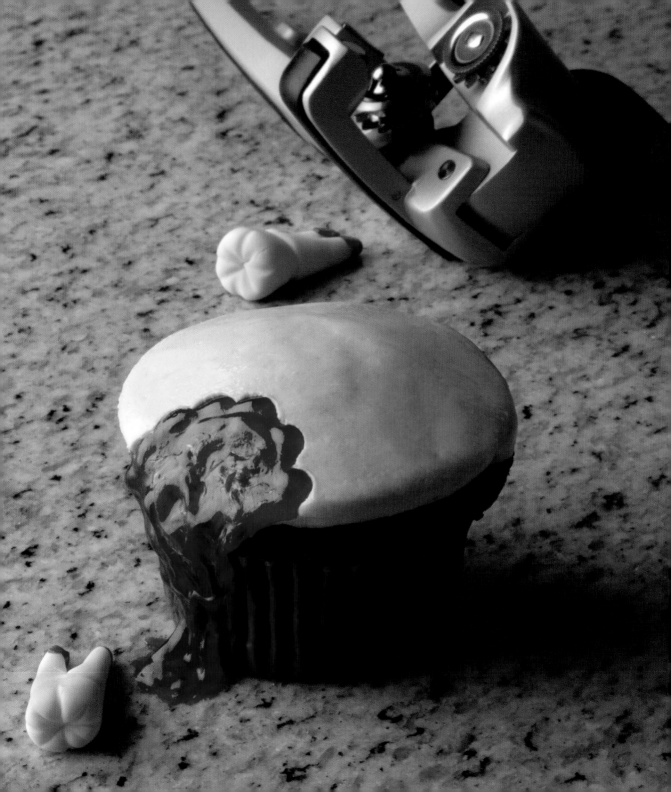

toxic bite

1 Preheat the oven to 375°F. Line a 12-hole muffin pan with 12 paper cupcake liners. Put the buttermilk, vanilla extract, vinegar, and red liquid food coloring in a bowl and mix together.

2 Put the butter and sugar in a large bowl and, using an electric mixer, beat together until pale and fluffy. Gradually add the eggs and beat well together. Sift in the flour, cocoa, baking soda, and salt and mix together. Add the buttermilk mixture and stir together until combined. Spoon the batter into the liners. Bake for about 20 minutes, turning once halfway through baking, until well risen and firm to the touch. Transfer to a wire rack and let cool.

3 Meanwhile, make the decorations. Add the peach food coloring to the Italian Meringue Buttercream in drops or on the end of a toothpick and mix well together until evenly colored. When the cupcakes are cool, spread or pipe the frosting on top of the cupcakes. (If you freeze the frosted cupcakes briefly, it will allow you to scrape the frosting very smoothly in steps 4 and 5.)

4 To create a bite on one side of each cupcake, begin by pressing the small end of a large plain piping tip into the frosting 5 to 7 times in a curve across the edge of the cake.

5 Use the piping tip to drag away some of the frosting in the bite area to create a lower level of frosting.

6 Fill in the bite with Piping Gel "Blood." Bring some of the gel down the side of the cupcake so that it forms a pool on the plate or table.

7 Use a toothpick to stir some of the buttercream into the gel in the middle of the bite to create a paler area.

8 Using a pastry bag or parchment paper cone fitted with a fine plain piping tip, pipe the remaining gel onto the root of each tooth and then lay the tooth in the pool of "blood" that has dripped off the cupcake.

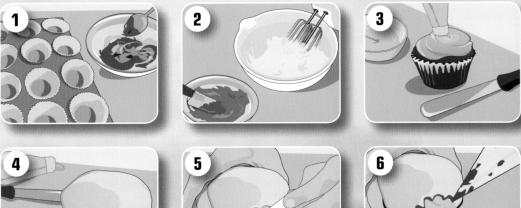

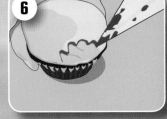

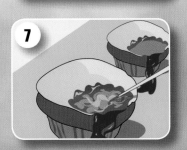

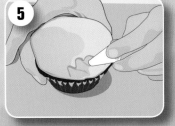

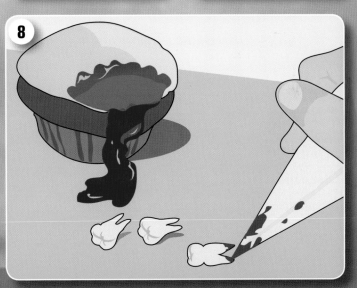

t-virus

DIFFICULTY RATING

MAKES **12**

Make the decorations the day before baking.

blue banana
cupcakes

- 1 very ripe banana
- 1 tsp lemon juice
- ½ cup (4 oz/1 stick) unsalted butter, softened
- 1 cup granulated sugar
- 3 large eggs, beaten
- ½ tsp grated lemon rind
- 2 tbsp sour cream
- 1 tsp blue liquid food coloring
- 1 tsp blue curaçao liqueur (optional)
- 1⅓ cups all-purpose, cake, or pastry flour
- 1 tsp baking powder
- ¼ tsp baking soda
- ¼ tsp salt

In the movie *Resident Evil* (2002), the cause of the zombie onslaught is the T-virus that is accidentally released, infecting the entire research facility where it was being developed. Dare to release this yummy cupcake version into your own system and see what happens. The recommended antidote, if you should need it, is a drop of green food coloring in a glass of cold milk.

decorations

- 3 oz plain white Half & Half (see page 11)
- 3½ oz Royal Icing, colored black with 8 drops black paste food coloring (see page 10)
- 1¾ oz Royal Icing, colored blue with 1 drop sky blue paste food coloring
- 1 quantity Italian Meringue Buttercream (see page 9)
- blue nonpareils, sugar strands, or other blue cake sprinkles

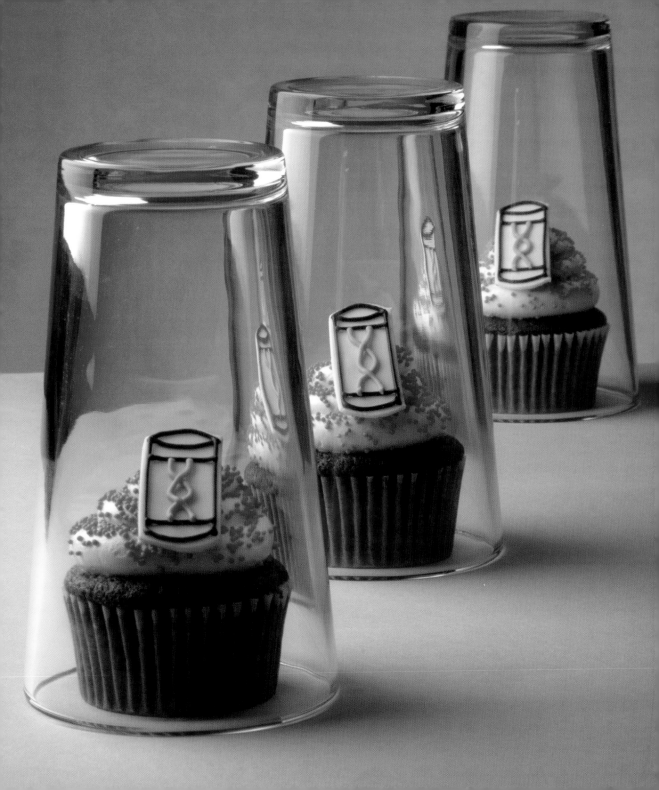

t-virus

1 The day before, make the decorations. Roll out the Half & Half to make the cupcake toppers using a strip of acetate 3 by 10 inches (see page 11). Using a craft knife (you can use a straight edge to steady the blade), cut the Half & Half into a strip 1½ inches wide.

2 Using the craft knife, cut the Half and Half strip at ¾-inch intervals to make 12 small rectangles.

3 Use the tip of the craft knife to cut off the corners of the rectangles and round the short edges into a curve.

4 Put the black Royal Icing in a pastry bag or parchment paper cone fitted with a fine plain piping tip and outline the vial. Add a curved line at the top, and a straight line near the top and the bottom. Repeat for the other vials.

5 Put the blue Royal Icing in a pastry bag or parchment paper cone fitted with a fine plain piping tip and pipe a squiggle down the center of the middle portion of the vial that curves right, left, and then right. Overlap that with a second squiggle that curves left, right, and left. Repeat for the other vials. Let dry, uncovered, overnight.

6 To make the cupcakes, preheat the oven to 350°F. Line a 12-hole muffin pan with 12 paper cupcake liners. Using a fork, mash the banana with the lemon juice. Put the butter and sugar in a large bowl and, using an electric mixer, beat together until pale and fluffy. Gradually add the eggs and beat well together.

7 Add the mashed banana, lemon rind, sour cream, blue food coloring, and blue curaçao, if using, and mix well together. Sift in the flour, baking powder, baking soda, and salt and mix together. Spoon the batter into the liners. Bake for about 20 minutes, turning once halfway through baking, until well risen and firm to the touch. Transfer to a wire rack and let cool.

8 When the cupcakes are cool, spread or pipe the Italian Meringue Buttercream on top of the cupcakes. Place the dry vials on top and sprinkle the entire remaining surface of the buttercream with the blue cake sprinkles.

know your zombie

Name the underground facility where the virus began to spread in *Resident Evil.*

1. The Vault

2. The Lair

3. The Hive

(The answer is on page 80.)

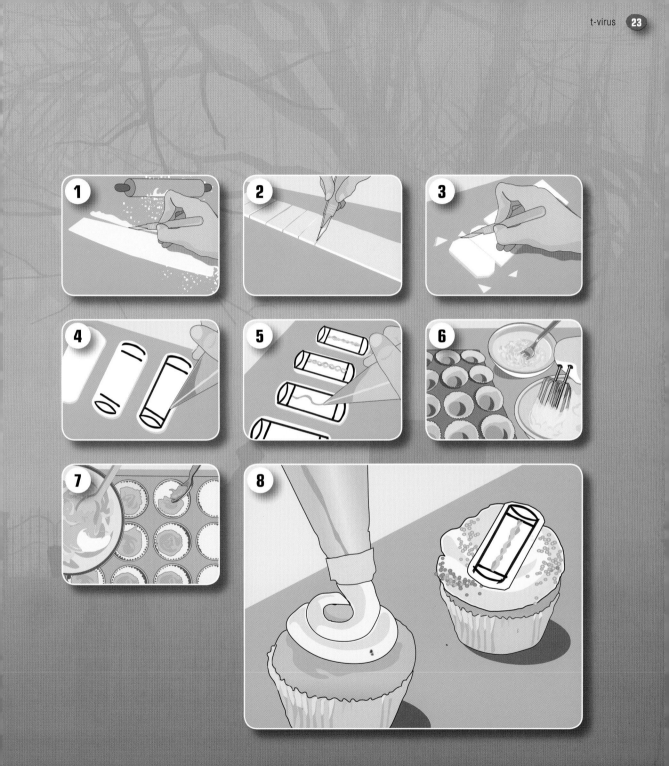

DIFFICULTY RATING

MAKES **12**

Make the decorations the day before baking.

key lime cupcakes

- 3 large eggs
- 2 tbsp vegetable oil
- grated rind of 1 lime and 2 tbsp juice
- 7 tbsp unsalted butter, softened
- 1 cup granulated sugar
- 2 tbsp sour cream
- 1½ cups all-purpose, cake, or pastry flour
- ½ tsp baking powder
- ¼ tsp salt

decorations

- 6 oz Half & Half, colored orange with 6 drops orange paste food coloring (see page 11)
- 1½ cups confectioners' sugar
- 2 tbsp lime juice
- 2 drops yellow paste food coloring
- 1 dab green paste food coloring

biohazard ingested

Proper disposal of biohazardous material is absolutely crucial to avoiding an outbreak of the undead. If there are zombies in your midst, someone hasn't been doing their job. Try this sensational key lime cupcake decorated with an orange biohazard symbol. But beware: post consumption, the consumer may have an eerie glow about them, indicating a shift toward the undead.

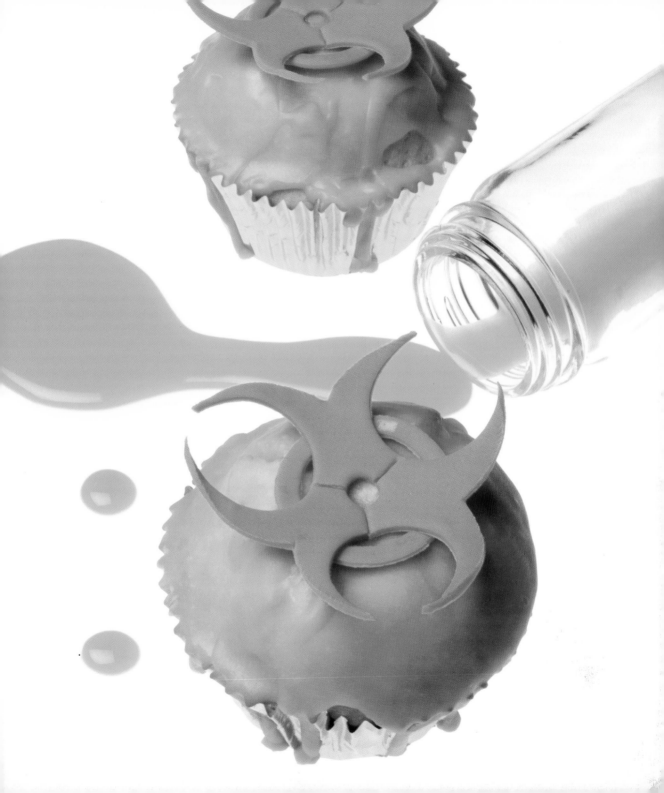

biohazard
ingested

1 The day before, make the decorations. Roll out a third of the Half & Half to make the cupcake toppers using a strip of acetate 3 by 8 inches (see page 11).

2 Using a 1¼-inch round cutter, cut a circle in the Half & Half. Using a ⅞-inch round cutter, cut a smaller circle inside the larger circle to make a narrow ring. This will be the center of the biohazard symbol. Repeat to cut out another 11 rings.

3 Make a template for the biohazard symbol using the photograph on page 25 for reference. Roll out the remaining Half & Half using 2 strips of acetate, each 3 by 16 inches (see page 11). Use the template to cut around the edge of the cluster of three circles. Using the ⅞-inch round cutter, make a hole in each larger circle that just overlaps the center of the curved edge.

4 Using the small end of a large plain piping tip, cut out a small hole in the center of the symbol. Using a toothpick, press a small indented line from the center circle toward the larger outer circle. Repeat to make another 11 symbols. Let the rings and symbols dry, uncovered, overnight.

5 Preheat the oven to 350°F. Line a 12-hole muffin pan with 12 paper cupcake liners. Put the eggs, oil, and lime rind and juice in a bowl and whisk together.

6 Put the butter and sugar in a large bowl and, using an electric mixer, beat together until pale and fluffy. Blend in the sour cream and then gradually beat in the egg mixture. Sift in the flour, baking powder, and salt and mix together. Spoon the batter into the liners. Bake for about 20 minutes, turning once halfway through baking, until well risen and firm to the touch. Transfer to a wire rack and let cool.

7 When the cupcakes are cool, make the glaze. Sift the confectioners' sugar into a large bowl and then gradually add the lime juice, stirring until the mixture is smooth and thick enough to coat the back of a wooden spoon. Add the yellow food coloring and, using the end of a toothpick, a dab of green food coloring and mix well together until evenly colored.

8 Dip each cupcake into the glaze so that it is liberally covered. Do not scrape off any extra glaze—drips down the side enhance the look of this cupcake. While the glaze is still wet, place a ring in the center of each cupcake. Rest a symbol on top of each ring.

know your zombie

The movie *The Serpent and the Rainbow* (1988) is based on the nonfiction book of the same name by which anthropologist?

1. Wade Davis

2. Margaret Mead

3. Nancy Scheper-Hughes

(The answer is on page 80.)

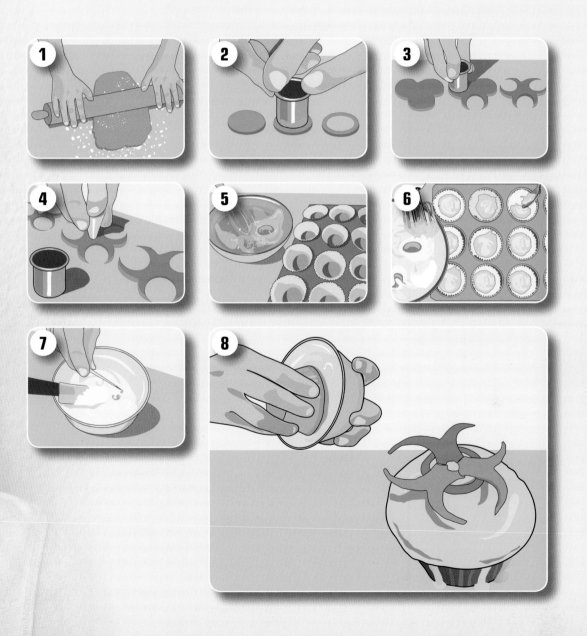

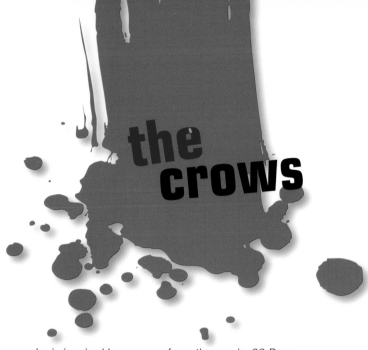

the crows

white velvet cupcakes

- 3 large egg whites
- ¾ cup milk
- ¾ tsp pure vanilla extract
- 2⅓ cups all-purpose, cake, or pastry flour
- 1 tbsp baking powder
- ¼ tsp salt
- 1 cup granulated sugar
- ½ cup plus 1 tbsp (4½ oz) unsalted butter, softened

decorations

- cornstarch, for dusting
- 12 oz store-bought fondant, colored flesh-colored with 1 to 2 drops peach and a dab of blue paste food coloring (see page 11)
- ½ cup seedless raspberry jam
- 12 oz Half & Half, colored black with 36 drops black paste food coloring (see page 11)
- 1 oz Royal Icing, colored red with 4 drops red paste food coloring (see page 10)
- 60 Maggots (see page 12)

This cupcake is inspired by a scene from the movie *28 Days Later*, where a crow sits overhead with a piece of zombie corpse in his mouth. We've chosen a deathly pale skin color, but you can vary the color of the fondant to create different flesh tones. The jam and fondant topping contrasts with the subtle flavor of the white velvet cupcake. If you use toothpicks to secure the crows, remember to tell your guests.

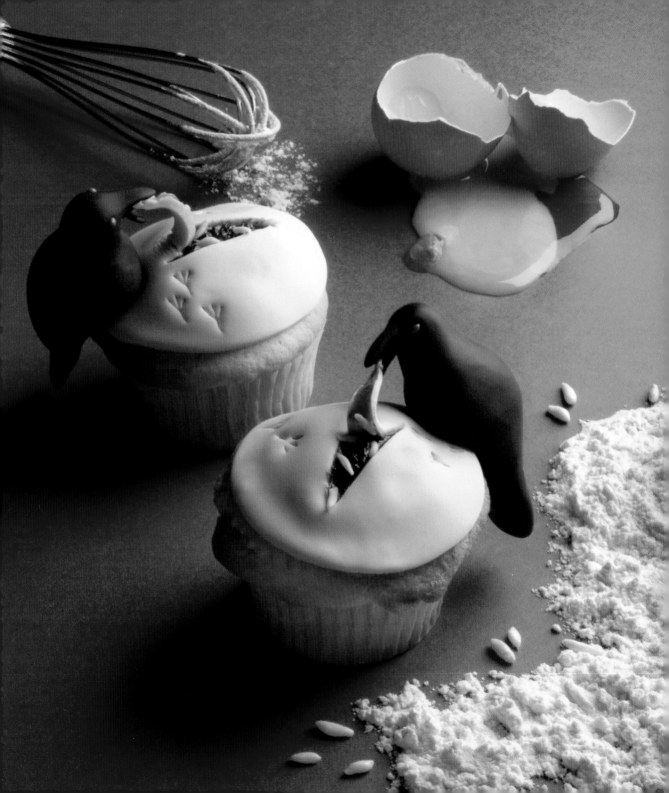

the crows

1 Preheat the oven to 350°F. Line a 12-hole muffin pan with 12 paper cupcake liners. Put the egg whites, 2 tablespoons of the milk, and the vanilla extract in a medium bowl and mix together with a fork.

2 Sift the flour, baking powder, and salt into a large bowl. Stir in the sugar. Add the butter and the remaining milk and, using an electric mixer, beat together until combined. Gradually beat in the egg white mixture. Spoon the batter into the liners. Bake for about 20 minutes, turning once halfway through baking, until well risen and firm to the touch. Transfer to a wire rack and let cool.

3 Dust the counter with cornstarch and roll out the fondant to a thickness of ⅛ inch. Using a 2½ to 3-inch round cutter, cut out 12 circles that will cover the cupcakes.

4 Use a teaspoon to create an indentation in the center of each cupcake and spoon 2 teaspoons raspberry jam into each. Cover each jam circle with a fondant circle.

5 To make the crows, divide the black Half & Half into 12 equal-size pieces. Reserving a tiny amount for the lower beak, roll one piece of the Half & Half into a ball. Squeeze and pinch the top of the ball to form the head. Squeeze, pinch, and flatten the other end of the ball to create the tail. From the head, squeeze and pinch out a long, pointy beak shape. Roll the reserved piece of Half & Half into another beak shape, but curving down at the tip. Attach below the upper beak with water, to make the beak appear open. Repeat to make another 11 crows.

6 With a craft knife, cut a long slit from just inside the edge of the fondant circle to ½ inch away from the edge on the opposite edge of the circle. Make a second cut that starts at the same point as the first and is the same length, but ends ¼ inch apart from the first cut.

7 Pull up the fondant strip to expose the raspberry jam below, then use water to attach the point of the strip to the inside of the crow's beak.

8 Attach the crow to the fondant circle with water. If necessary, anchor the crow to the cupcake with a small piece of toothpick. Using a pastry bag or parchment paper cone fitted with a fine plain piping tip, pipe red Royal Icing eyes onto the crow. Use a craft knife to score crow footprints on the fondant. Place the Maggots in the raspberry jam. Repeat to decorate the remaining cupcakes.

know your zombie

What happens after 28 days in the movie *28 Days Later*?

1. The zombies start to die of starvation

2. The survivors start to mutate into zombies

3. The zombies turn on each other

(The answer is on page 80.)

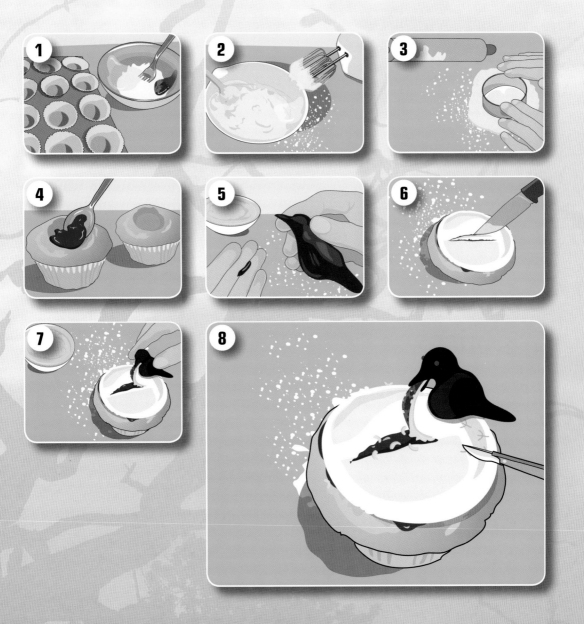

devil's food cupcakes

- 4 tbsp (2 oz/½ stick) unsalted butter, softened
- ¾ cup plus 2 tbsp firmly packed dark brown sugar
- 2 large eggs
- ⅔ cup all-purpose, cake, or pastry flour
- ¾ tsp baking soda
- ¼ cup unsweetened cocoa
- ¼ tsp salt
- ½ cup sour cream

decorations

- 3 drops brown paste food coloring
- 3 drops black paste food coloring
- cornstarch, for dusting
- 6½ oz store-bought fondant, colored yellow with 3 drops lemon yellow paste food coloring (see page 11)
- lemon extract or vodka, for thinning
- ½ quantity Dark Chocolate Ganache (see page 8)

zombie moon

Your worst nightmare has come true: the zombies are out; they are about to take over the night and they are very hungry. Here they come from behind every gravestone, gnarled tree, and fallen cross. Each cupcake is decorated with a zombie rising from the grave, silhouetted against a full moon. This rich devil's food cupcake will help you recognize the enemy and give you the energy to run for your life.

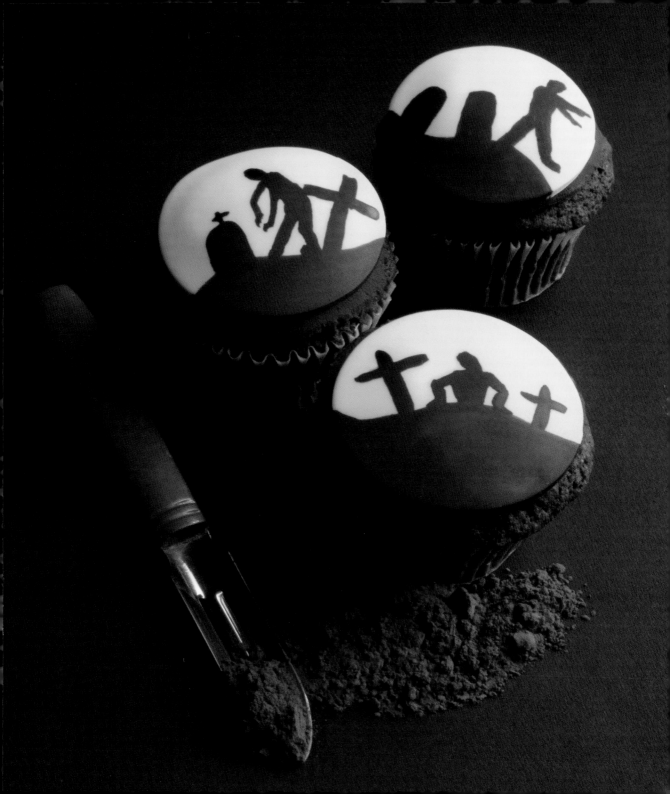

zombie moon

1 The day before, make the decorations. Put the brown and black food colorings in drops or on the end of a toothpick onto the lid of an empty jar or plastic container with a raised lip. Mix together with a toothpick and set aside.

2 Dust the counter with cornstarch and roll out the fondant to a thickness of ⅛ inch.

3 Using a 2½ to 3-inch round cutter, cut out 12 circles that will cover the cupcakes.

4 Pour a small amount of lemon extract or vodka onto the dried food coloring to thin it and mix with a small paintbrush to a painting consistency. Using the photograph on page 33 for inspiration, paint zombies, rolling hills, gravestones, and crosses on the yellow fondant circles. Let the paint dry.

5 To make the cupcakes, preheat the oven to 350°F. Line a 12-hole muffin pan with 12 paper cupcake liners. Put the butter, sugar, eggs, flour, baking soda, cocoa, and salt in a large bowl and, using an electric mixer, beat together until smooth.

6 Add the sour cream to the mixture and fold in with a large wooden spoon until combined. Spoon the batter into the liners. Bake for 20 to 25 minutes, turning once halfway through baking, until well risen and firm to the touch. Transfer to a wire rack and let cool.

7 When the cupcakes are cool, using a pastry bag or parchment paper cone fitted with a large plain piping tip, pipe a swirl of Dark Chocolate Ganache onto one cupcake.

8 Smooth the swirl with a palette knife or spatula. Place a fondant disk on top of the ganache. Repeat for the remaining cupcakes. Display the cupcakes in a row, to create the illusion of many zombies roaming a graveyard.

know your zombie

The 1943 movie *I Walked with a Zombie* is loosely based on which novel?

1. *Jane Eyre* by Charlotte Brontë (1847)

2. *Frankenstein* by Mary Shelley (1818)

3. *The Premature Burial* by Edgar Allan Poe (1844)

(The answer is on page 80.)

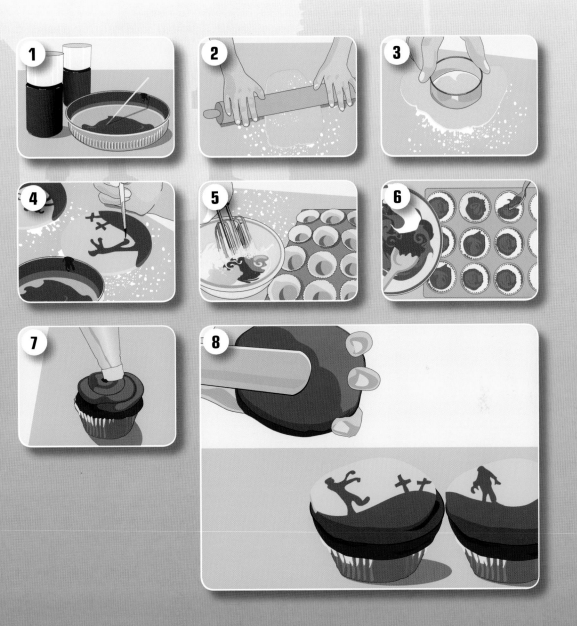

DIFFICULTY RATING

MAKES **12**

Make the decorations the day before baking.

mud cupcakes

- 10 Oreo cookies
- 1¾ oz semisweet chocolate
- 1 cup all-purpose, cake, or pastry flour
- ¼ tsp baking soda
- ¼ tsp salt
- 5 tbsp unsalted butter, softened
- ¾ cup granulated sugar
- 2 large eggs, beaten
- ½ tsp pure vanilla extract
- 2 tbsp sour cream
- 2 tbsp water
- ½ cup mini semisweet chocolate chips

decorations

- 12½ oz Half & Half, colored green with 1 drop mint green paste food coloring (see page 11)
- 1 quantity Dark Chocolate Ganache (see page 9)
- 1 cup finely crushed chocolate cookies
- ⅔ cup mini semisweet chocolate chips
- a little clear piping gel
- 12 Flies (see page 14)

zombies rising

Take a close look at a graveyard, and you might see a zombie rising from the dead—if you see a rotting hand reaching out from underground, you can be sure the rest of the zombie will soon follow. They're coming to get you … This delectable mud cupcake gives you a taste of the grave from the zombie's perspective. Remember to warn your guests that the hand is secured using a toothpick.

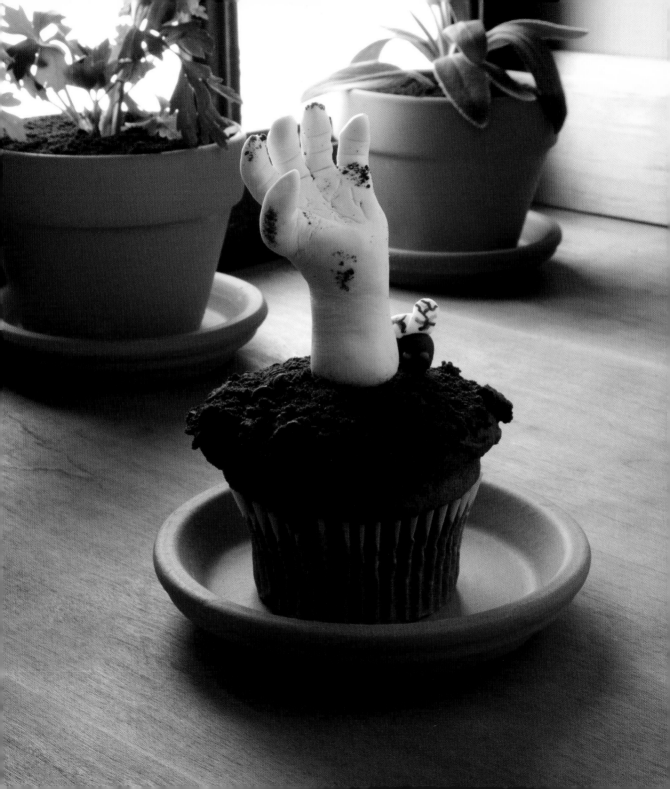

zombies rising

1 The day before, make the hands. Roll the green Half & Half into 12 balls and then roll and press one end of each ball to thin it out into a cylinder shape. Flatten the rounded end so that the piece of frosting vaguely resembles a Ping-Pong paddle.

2 Using a craft knife, make one cut on one side of the flattened area to make a thumb. Pull it out to the side. Make a second cut in the middle of the remaining rounded portion, and a third and fourth cut on either side to create 4 fingers.

3 Pull and mold the tips of the fingers to make them slightly pointed. Using a toothpick, score 3 lines into each finger to create joints. This will be the palm side of the hand. On the reverse side, use the toothpick to indent a fingernail shape at the end of each finger.

4 Bend the fingers up from the palm to resemble a claw. Prop the hand against a vertical surface so that it dries in the claw shape. Make another 11 hands in the same way and let dry, uncovered, overnight.

5 Preheat the oven to 350°F. Line a 12-hole muffin pan with 12 cupcake liners. Crush the Oreo cookies into ¼-inch pieces. Spoon 1 tablespoon into each liner, reserving the remaining pieces.

6 Melt the chocolate in a microwave oven on low, stirring every 15 seconds, or in a heatproof bowl set over a saucepan of gently simmering water, stirring occasionally. Remove from the heat and let cool. Sift the flour, baking soda, and salt together and set aside. Put the butter and sugar in a large bowl and, using an electric mixer, beat together until pale and fluffy. Blend in the melted chocolate and then gradually beat in the eggs and mix well together. Mix in the vanilla extract and sour cream. Add half the flour mixture and blend in, then mix in the water and remaining flour mixture until incorporated.

7 Spoon half the batter into the liners and spread over the cookies. Add 1 heaping teaspoon of chocolate chips to each. Add the remaining batter and sprinkle the remaining chocolate chips and cookie pieces over the tops. Bake for about 25 minutes, turning once halfway through baking, until well risen and firm to the touch. Transfer to a wire rack and let cool.

8 When the cupcakes are cool, spread or pipe the Dark Chocolate Ganache on top of each cupcake. Mix together most of the chocolate cookie crumbs and all of the chocolate chips in a dish and dip the top of each cupcake into the mixture to create graveyard earth.

9 Push a toothpick into the wrist end of each hand and press it into the earth to anchor it. To enhance the effect of the hand rising from the grave, paint clear piping gel in different places on the hand and at the base, and sprinkle the remaining chocolate cookie crumbs on the gel so that it sticks. Finish by adding a Fly.

know your zombie

Who directed the 2004 remake of George A. Romero's *Dawn of the Dead*?

1. David Cronenberg

2. Zack Snyder

3. Tom Savini

(The answer is on page 80.)

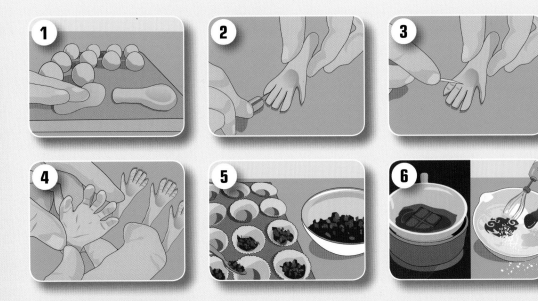

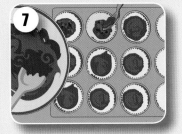

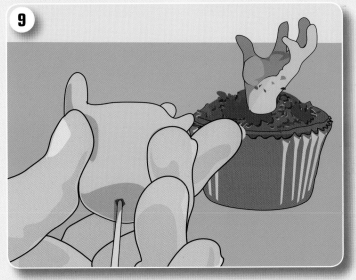

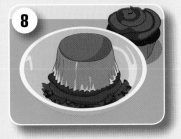

trick or treat

DIFFICULTY RATING

MAKES **24**

Make the decorations the day before baking.

vanilla cupcakes

- ½ cup (4 oz/1 stick) unsalted butter, softened
- 1 cup granulated sugar
- 3 large eggs, beaten
- ⅔ cup milk
- 1 tsp pure vanilla extract
- 1½ cups all-purpose, cake, or pastry flour
- 1½ tsp baking powder
- ¼ tsp salt

chocolate cupcakes

- ½ cup (4 oz/1 stick) unsalted butter, softened
- 1 cup granulated sugar
- 3 large eggs, beaten
- ⅔ cup milk
- ½ tsp pure vanilla extract
- 1⅓ cups all-purpose, cake, or pastry flour
- ¼ cup unsweetened cocoa
- 1½ tsp baking powder
- ¼ tsp salt

"Trick or treat, smell my feet, give me something good to eat." Sure, kid, here you go! Feeling lucky? You've got about an 80 percent chance of receiving the treat. If not, better luck next time. Remember to give anyone who bites into a trick one a treat afterward. We've combined the vanilla and chocolate cupcakes to make layered cupcakes, but you could instead make separate batches of single-flavor cupcakes.

filling

- 20 large marshmallows
- 2 tbsp butter or margarine
- a little cold mashed potato

decorations

- cornstarch, for dusting
- 1½ lbs store-bought white fondant
- 9 oz Piping Gel "Blood" (see page 10)
- 24 assorted candies
- Rat, Knife, Tooth, and Fly (see pages 12 and 14; optional)

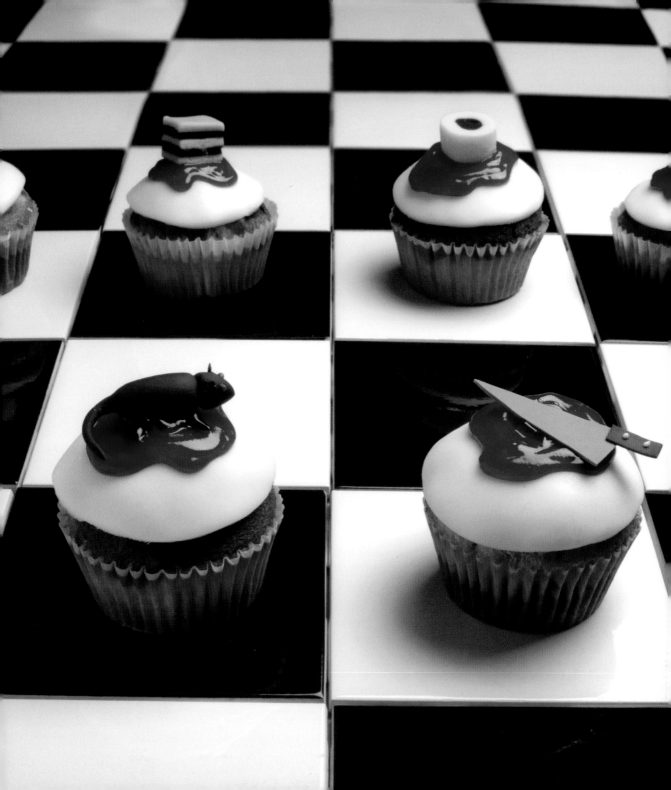

trick or treat

1 Preheat the oven to 350°F. Line two 12-hole muffin pans with 24 paper cupcake liners. To make the Vanilla Cupcakes, put the butter and sugar in a large bowl and, using an electric mixer, beat together until pale and fluffy.

2 Gradually beat the eggs into the mixture, and then stir in the milk and vanilla extract. Sift in the flour, baking powder, and salt and fold into the mixture with a large metal spoon. Spoon half of the batter into 12 of the liners and reserve the remainder.

3 To make the Chocolate Cupcakes, put the butter and sugar in a large bowl and, using an electric mixer, beat together until pale and fluffy. Gradually beat in the eggs, and then stir in the milk and vanilla extract. Sift in the flour, cocoa, baking powder, and salt and fold into the mixture with a large wooden spoon.

4 Spoon half of the batter into the liners, on top of the vanilla batter. Spoon the other half into the remaining 12 liners and top with the reserved vanilla batter. Bake for about 25 minutes, turning once halfway through baking, until well risen and firm to the touch. Transfer to a wire rack and let cool.

5 To fill the cupcakes, use a teaspoon to scoop out a 1-inch plug from the center of each cupcake and set aside for later. Use the teaspoon to remove a little more cake from the holes to make room for the filling.

6 To make the "treat" filling, put the marshmallows and butter or margarine in a saucepan and heat gently, stirring constantly, until melted. Let cool for 5 minutes, then pour the warm mixture into a 12-inch disposable pastry bag. Pipe the mixture into 20 of the cupcakes. For the "trick" filling, spoon a little mashed potato into the holes of the remaining 4 cupcakes. Replace a reserved cake plug over each filled hole.

7 To decorate the cupcakes, dust the counter with cornstarch and roll out the fondant to a thickness of ⅛ inch. Using a 2½ to 3-inch round cutter, cut out 24 circles to cover the cupcakes.

8 Fit a pastry bag or parchment paper cone with a fine plain piping tip and fill with the Piping Gel "Blood." Squeeze the gel into the center of each fondant circle, smearing and dripping as you wish.

9 Place assorted candies in the pools of gel. If desired, a Rat, Knife, Tooth, and Fly can also look very effective when added to a few of the cupcakes.

know your zombie

What is the name of Shaun and Ed's favorite pub in the movie *Shaun of the Dead* (2004)?

1. The Duke of Albany

2. The Winchester

3. The King's Head

(The answer is on page 80.)

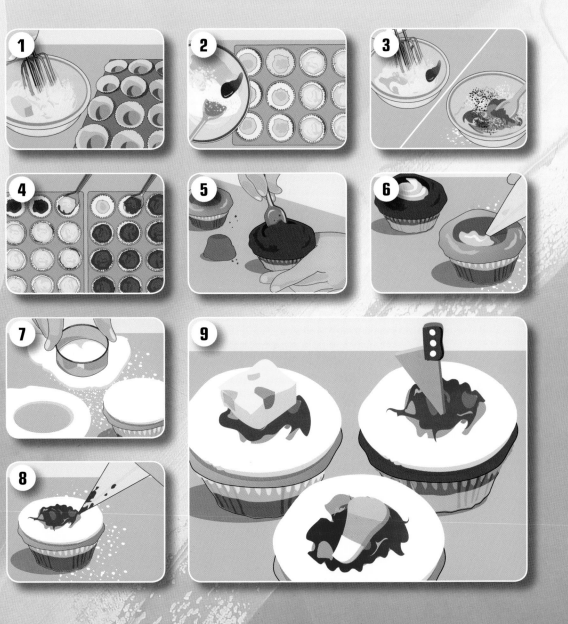

on the
loose

DIFFICULTY RATING

MAKES **12**

Make the decorations the day
before baking.

applesauce & caramel cupcakes

- ½ cup (4 oz/1 stick) unsalted butter, softened
- 1¼ cups firmly packed light brown sugar
- 2 large eggs, beaten
- 3 cups all-purpose, cake, or pastry flour
- ½ tsp baking soda
- 1½ tsp ground cinnamon
- ¼ tsp ground cloves
- ¼ tsp salt
- ½ cup applesaucer
- 1 Granny Smith apple, peeled, cored, and finely chopped
- 12 soft caramels or soft toffees

You can chain a zombie down, but there is no guarantee it will stay put for long. With rotten body parts liable to fall off anyway, being a leg down won't worry a zombie if it allows it to escape. This delectable apple cupcake with a caramel or toffee center begs the question, "The foot's still here, but where has the rest of my zombie gone?"

decorations

- 12½ oz Half & Half, colored green with 1 drop pale green paste food coloring (see page 11)
- 2 oz plain white Half & Half
- 1 lb 5 oz Half & Half, colored gray with 1 drop black paste food coloring
- cornstarch, for dusting
- 1 quantity Cream Cheese Frosting (see page 10)
- ¾ oz Piping Gel "Blood" (see page 10)

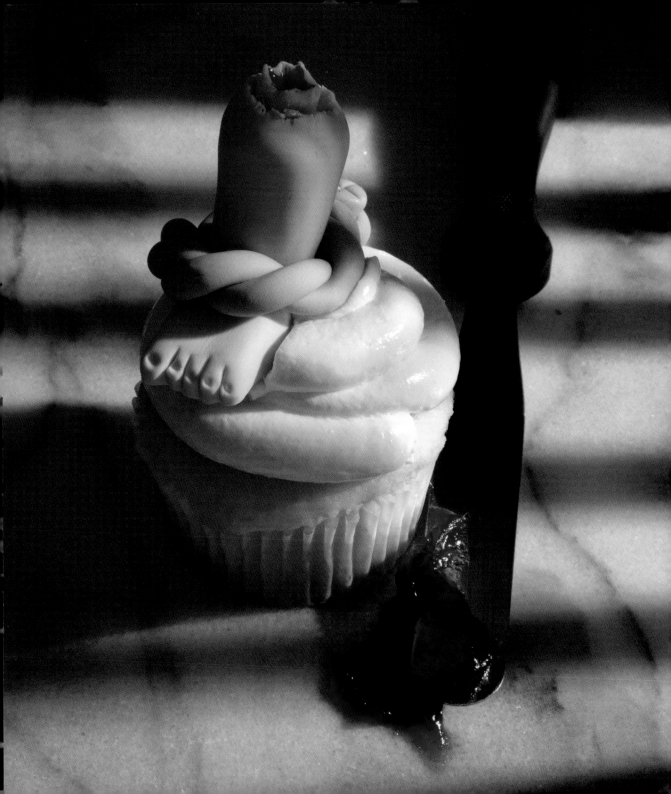

on the loose

1 The day before, make the decorations. To make the foot and leg, roll the pale green Half & Half into 12 balls and use your fingers to roll each ball into a thick log. Bend one end at a 90-degree angle. Pinch and push the bent end into the shape of a foot, pressing the toes flat.

2 Use a craft knife to make a cut at one end of the foot to create the big toe. Cut a small amount off the top of the remaining foot shape to make it slightly shorter. Make 3 cuts at even intervals to create toes. Use a toothpick to indent toenail shapes into the tip of each toe.

3 Make a hole in the top of each leg with the handle of a wooden spoon, then use a toothpick to tear at the hole to make it look severed. Divide the white Half & Half in two. On a counter dusted with cornstarch, roll each piece into a long sausage shape slightly smaller in diameter than the wooden spoon's handle. Cut each sausage into 6 short, equal lengths and use water to attach one inside each leg to look like exposed bone. Make a slight indentation at the end of the bone for marrow.

4 To make the chains, divide 1 lb 2 oz of the gray Half & Half into 12 equal-size pieces, then roll each piece into a ball and then into a 10-inch-long, thin sausage shape. Fold in half, hold one end and twist the 2 lengths together to create a chain.

5 Loop a chain around each foot, leaving one end overlapping the other by ½ inch, and attach them together with water. Press the ½-inch overlap flat and use the small end of a large plain piping tip to cut a hole in the center to allow for a nail.

6 To make the nails, divide the remaining gray Half & Half in half and then roll each half into a long sausage shape thin enough to fit the chain holes. Cut each sausage into 6 short, equal lengths. Press one end of one short length onto the counter to create a flat top. Use a toothpick to score a line across the top, and then make a second score perpendicular to the first. Push the nail through the chain hole. Repeat with the remaining lengths. Let the decorations dry, uncovered, overnight.

7 Preheat the oven to 350°F. Line a 12-hole muffin pan with 12 paper cupcake liners. Put the butter and sugar in a large bowl and, using an electric mixer, beat together until combined. Gradually beat in the eggs. Sift in the flour, baking soda, spices, and salt and fold them in. Fold in the applesauce and chopped apple.

8 Spoon half the batter into the liners. Place a caramel or toffee in each and then spoon the remaining mixture on top. Bake for about 25 minutes, turning once halfway through baking, until well risen and firm to the touch. Transfer to a wire rack and let cool.

9 Not long before serving, frost the cupcakes with the Cream Cheese Frosting. Place a foot, chain, and nail on top of each frosted cupcake. Using a pastry bag or parchment paper cone fitted with a fine plain piping tip, pipe Piping Gel "Blood" in the center of the bone and at the edge of the ripped skin to enhance the appearance of a severed limb.

know your zombie

Father McGruder says which of the following in *Dead Alive* (1992)?

1. "I kick ass for the Lord!"

2. "I preach for the Lord!"

3. "I teach for the Lord!"

(The answer is on page 80.)

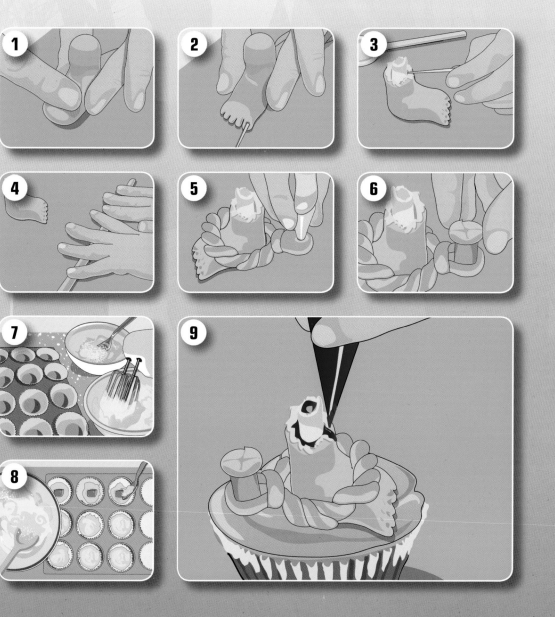

carrot
cupcakes

- ⅔ cup vegetable oil
- 3 large eggs
- ¾ cup plus 2 tbsp granulated sugar
- 1 tsp pure vanilla extract
- 1⅓ cups all-purpose, cake, or pastry flour
- 1½ tsp baking soda
- 1½ tsp ground cinnamon
- ½ tsp ground allspice
- ½ tsp grated nutmeg
- ¼ tsp salt
- 1½ cups grated carrots
- ⅓ cup chopped walnuts
- ½ cup canned crushed pineapple

zombies'
delights

Zombies deserve a treat every now and then. So serve them
up some of these irresistible organ-laden carrot cupcakes and
they might not even notice that they are not real body parts.
Hopefully, this will give you just a few extra minutes to escape
with your own organs intact. For an even wider selection of parts,
you could serve these alongside the Brain Food (see page 60)
and the Eye Poppers (see page 56).

decorations

- 5½ oz Half & Half, colored pink with 1 drop
  soft pink paste food coloring (see page 11)
- 1 oz Royal Icing, colored peach with ½ drop
  peach paste food coloring (see page 10)
- 1 oz red Royal Icing, colored red with 4 drops
  red paste food coloring
- 1 oz Royal Icing, colored blue with 5 drops
  royal blue paste food coloring

- cornstarch, for dusting
- 4 oz store-bought fondant, colored red
  with 4 drops super red paste food coloring
  (see page 11)
- 4 oz store-bought fondant, colored black with
  8 drops black paste food coloring
- 4 oz store-bought fondant, colored purple
  with 6 drops regal purple paste food coloring
- 3 oz clear piping gel

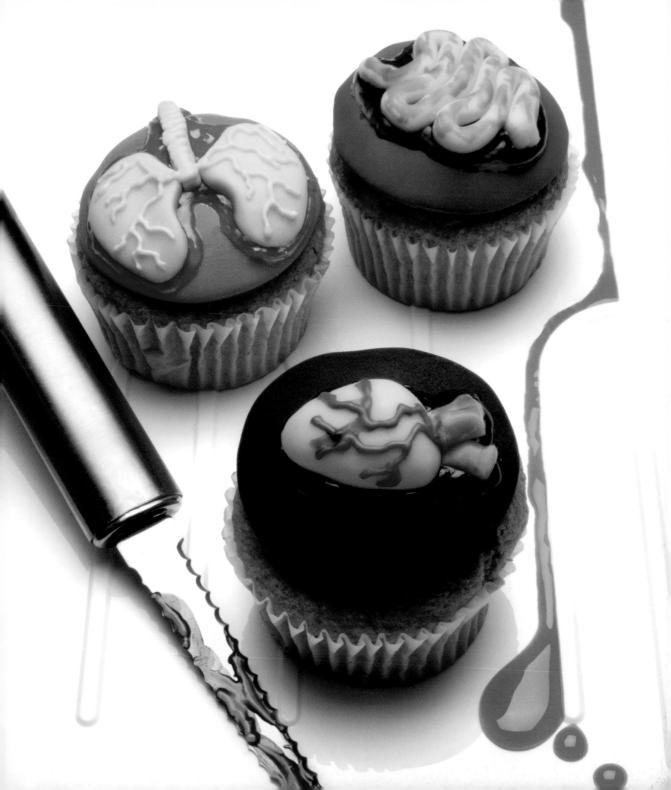

zombies' delights

1 The day before, make 4 lungs, 4 hearts, and 4 intestines. For lungs, roll 2 oz of the pink Half & Half into a ball. Flatten to a disk and cut in half. Squeeze and pinch one inside corner of each half to make lung shaped. Place so that they are almost touching on a sheet of acetate. To make the trachea, roll ½ oz of the pink Half & Half into a ball and then into a small sausage shape. Use a little water to attach it to the lungs.

2 Fit a pastry bag or parchment paper cone with a fine plain piping tip and fill with the peach Royal Icing. Pipe branch shapes on the lungs to look like bronchial tubes, and pipe lines on the trachea.

3 For hearts, roll 2 oz of the pink Half & Half into a ball. Cut a third off to make the valves. Squeeze the larger amount into a rounded triangle shape for the heart. Roll the smaller amount into a thin sausage and cut into thirds. Use a little water to attach the valves to the top of the heart.

4 Fit 2 pastry bags or parchment paper cones with fine plain piping tips and fill one with the red Royal Icing and the other with the blue Royal Icing. Pipe red and blue branching lines on the heart to appear like veins and arteries.

5 For intestines, roll 1 oz of the pink Half & Half into a ball and then into a long, thin sausage. Curve into a squiggly mass, with one end pointing up and one end pointing

down, like the beginning and the end of small intestines. Pipe a little red Royal Icing on top and paint with water to thin it. Let the organs dry, uncovered, overnight.

6 Preheat the oven to 350°F. Line a 12-hole muffin pan with 12 paper cupcake liners. Put the oil, eggs, sugar, and vanilla extract in a large bowl and, using an electric mixer, beat together until combined and smooth.

7 Sift in the flour, baking soda, spices, and salt and then mix together. Stir in the carrots, walnuts, and pineapple. Spoon the batter into the liners. Bake for about 25 minutes, turning once halfway through baking, until well risen and firm to the touch. Transfer to a wire rack and let cool.

8 To decorate, on a counter dusted with cornstarch, roll out the red, black, and purple fondant. Using a 2½ to 3-inch round cutter, cut out 4 circles of each and use them to cover the cupcakes. Use a little water to attach the lungs to the red circles, the hearts to the black circles, and the intestines to the purple circles.

9 Fit a pastry bag or parchment paper cone with a fine plain piping tip and fill with clear piping gel. Pipe the gel all around the edge of each organ to make them appear as if they are oozing.

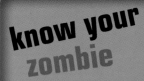

know your zombie

Seth Grahame-Smith's 2009 book adds zombies to which Jane Austen novel?

1. *Sense and Sensibility*

2. *Mansfield Park*

3. *Pride and Prejudice*

(The answer is on page 80.)

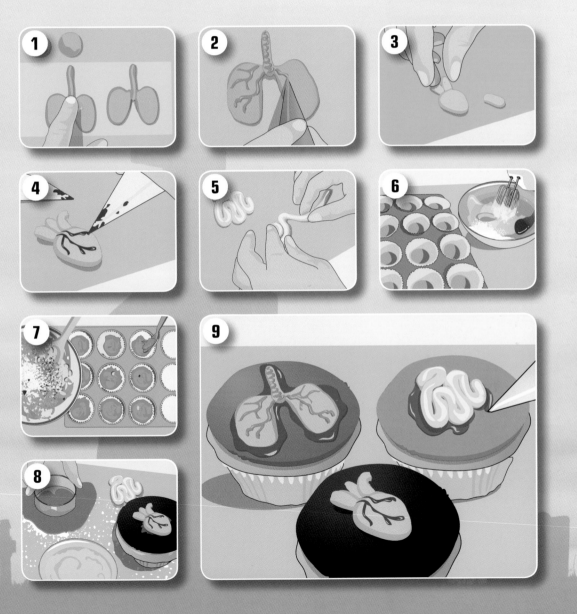

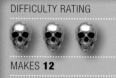

DIFFICULTY RATING

MAKES **12**

Make the decorations the day before baking.

bride & groom

bride's cupcakes

- 1 quantity Vanilla Cupcakes
  (see Trick or Treat, page 40)

decorations

- 4 oz white couverture chocolate
- 24 mini shortbread cookies
- 2 oz Half & Half, colored black with 4 drops black paste food coloring (see page 11)
- 1¾ oz Royal Icing, colored black with 4 drops black paste food coloring (see page 10)
- 1¾ oz Royal Icing, colored yellow with 1 drop yellow paste food coloring
- 48 white sugar pearls or a little plain white Royal Icing
- 1½ oz Piping Gel "Blood" (see page 10)
- 12 large marshmallows
- 2 lbs 10 oz plain white Half & Half
- cornstarch, for dusting
- 1 oz plain white Royal Icing
- 12 Knives (see page 15)

Even zombies are looking for a match made in heaven (well, hell). These two might have found rotting, decrepit love in each other's bloodshot empty eyes, if only the bride could have controlled herself just a little bit longer. Snack on the groom's head before taking a bite out of the scrumptious bride yourself. Retribution is only fair. The bride is made up of an upside-down cupcake with a marshmallow upper body and a shortbread head, all secured using a bamboo skewer (remember to let your guests know). Her dress is white Half & Half; don't worry if you tear it—the old superstition about it meaning the marriage will be ended by death doesn't really apply here.

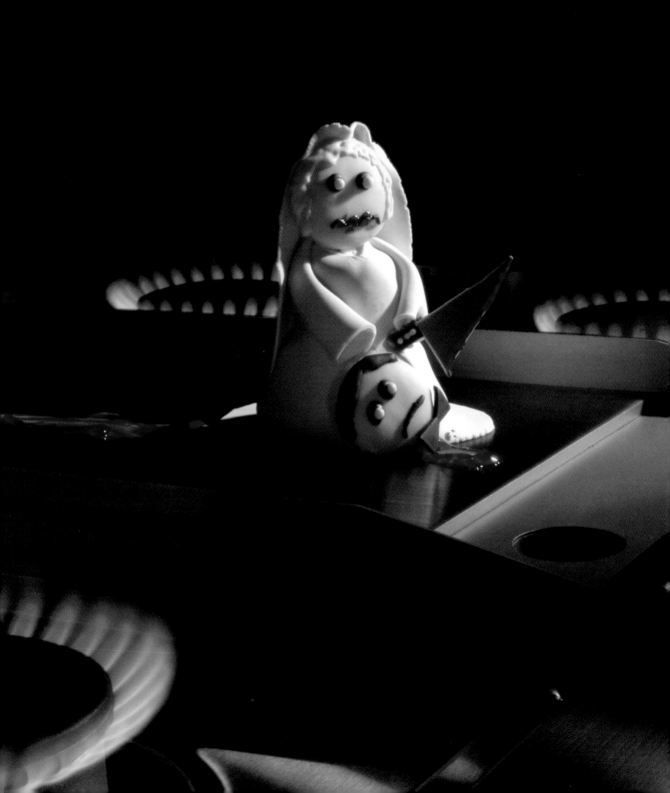

bride & groom

1 Preheat the oven to 350°F. Line a 12-hole muffin pan with 12 paper cupcake liners. Make the Vanilla Cupcakes as described in steps 1 and 2 on page 42, but divide all of the batter between the 12 liners. Transfer to a wire rack and let cool completely overnight.

2 To make the decorations, melt the white chocolate in a microwave oven on low, stirring every 15 seconds, or in a heatproof bowl set over a saucepan of gently simmering water, stirring occasionally. Attach a 4-inch-long bamboo skewer to the back of 12 shortbread cookies with a small amount of the melted chocolate. When set, turn the cookies over and spoon the chocolate over the surface to coat evenly. Coat a second set of 12 cookies, without sticks, for the groom. Let set. Roll out the black Half & Half to make the grooms' ties (see page 11) using a strip of acetate 3 by 3 inches. Cut out 2 small triangles to make each tie. Let dry on the acetate.

3 Fit pastry bags or parchment paper cones with fine plain piping tips, fill with the black and yellow Royal Icing, and use to pipe the faces and hair on the bride and groom. Place a white sugar pearl or a small dot of white Royal Icing in the center of each black eye to create an eyeball. When set, use Piping Gel "Blood" to pipe around the bride's mouth.

4 To make the bride's body, remove the cupcakes from their liners and level the tops with a serrated knife. Turn the cupcakes upside down and place a marshmallow on top of each. Push a bamboo skewer with a cookie attached through the marshmallow into each cupcake until the cookie rests on the marshmallow.

5 To make the bride's dress, roll 2 oz of the white Half & Half into a ball. On a counter dusted with cornstarch, roll out the ball into a rectangle with rounded edges, measuring about 3½ by 8½ inches. Wrap the rectangle around the bride so that it overlaps at the back and attach with water. Use a craft knife to trim the front so that it tucks under the bride's chin and the base so that it just touches the ground. If desired, make cuts and scrapes in the dress so that it appears tattered.

6 To make the sleeves, roll out 1½ oz of the white Half & Half into an oval about 6 by 2½ by 4 inches. Cut the oval in half—the straight edges will become the cuffs. Form each half into a cone, leaving a round opening at the wide end. Use water to attach the sides together. Brush water down the seam of each sleeve and attach to the dress. Press the closed end of the sleeve firmly down around the back of the bride.

7 Use white Royal Icing to attach a Knife to one of the sleeves. Pipe Piping Gel "Blood" on the knife. If desired, use white Royal Icing to pipe details on the dress.

8 To make the veil, roll out 1 oz of the white Half & Half very thinly to an oval about 3 by 5½ inches. Gather one end together into small pleats and secure the pleats with a little water. Brush water on the back of the pleats, in the center, and attach the veil to the back of the bride's head so that some of the veil extends above her head. If desired, tatter the veil with a craft knife. Repeat steps 5 to 8 to make 11 more brides.

9 To assemble, place the bride on the intended display surface. Use white Royal Icing to attach the groom's head to the side of the bride's skirt. Use black Royal Icing to attach the groom's tie to his severed neck. Use Piping Gel "Blood" to create a pool of blood beneath his tie. Repeat to make the other 11 couples.

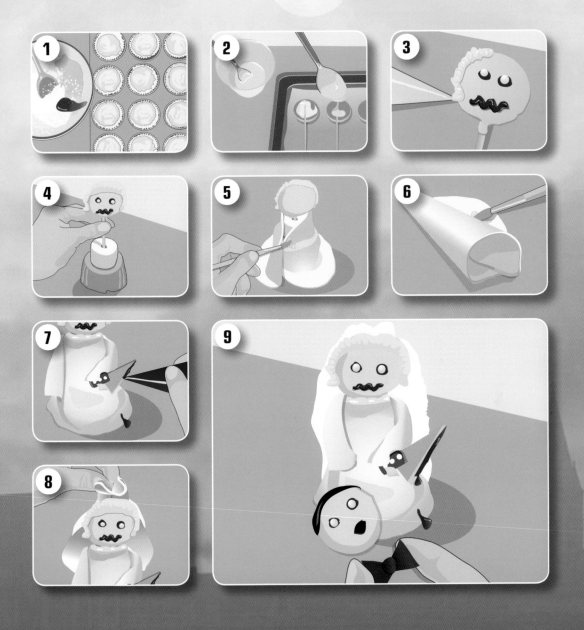

DIFFICULTY RATING

MAKES **12**

Decorations can be made the same day as baking.

eye poppers

almond cupcakes

- 2 large eggs
- ½ cup sour cream
- 1 tsp almond extract
- ¼ tsp pure vanilla extract
- pink paste food coloring
- 1⅔ cups all-purpose, cake, or pastry flour
- ½ tsp baking powder
- ½ tsp baking soda
- ¼ tsp salt
- ¼ cup finely ground almonds
- ¾ cup plus 2 tbsp granulated sugar
- ¾ cup (6 oz/1½ sticks) unsalted butter, softened

In most cases, it is all fun and games until someone loses an eye. This delightfully gory yet delicious almond cupcake is the exception that proves the rule. Be sure to save the eyeball for last to make all your zombie friends jealous as you savor its sweetness. You can replace the blue Half & Half with other colors to vary the colors of the eyes.

decorations

- cornstarch, for dusting
- 12 oz store-bought fondant, colored flesh-color with 2 to 3 drops peach paste food coloring (see page 11)
- 6 oz plain white Half & Half (see page 11)
- 6 oz Half & Half, colored brown with 10 drops brown and 1 drop black paste food coloring
- ½ oz Half & Half, colored blue with 1 drop sky blue paste food coloring
- ¼ oz Half & Half, colored black with 1 drop black paste food coloring
- red edible marker pen
- 3 oz Piping Gel "Blood" (see page 10)

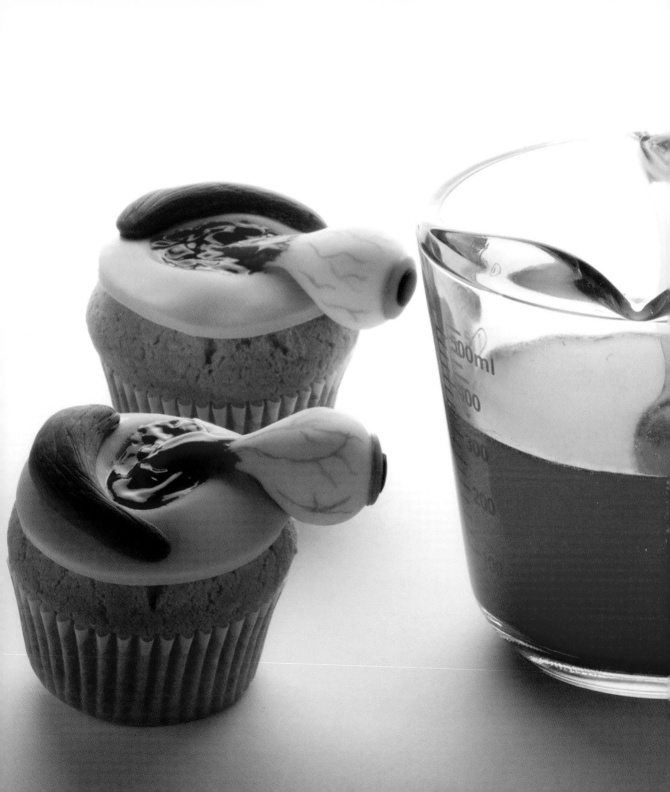

eye poppers

1 Preheat the oven to 350°F. Line a 12-hole muffin pan with 12 paper cupcake liners. Put the eggs, 3 tablespoons of the sour cream, and the almond and vanilla extracts in a bowl and mix together. Add pink food coloring in drops or on the end of a toothpick and mix well together until evenly colored deep pink.

2 Sift the flour, baking powder, baking soda, and salt into a large bowl. Stir in the almonds and sugar. Add the butter and remaining sour cream and, using an electric mixer, beat together until combined. Gradually beat in the egg mixture until combined. Spoon the batter into the liners. Bake for about 20 minutes, turning once halfway through baking, until well risen and firm to the touch. Transfer to a wire rack and let cool.

3 When the cupcakes are cool, use your thumb to press an eye socket shape into the top of each.

4 Dust the counter with cornstarch and roll out the fondant to a thickness of 1/8 inch. Using a 2½ to 3-inch round cutter, cut out 12 circles that will cover the cupcakes. Press one onto the top of each cupcake.

5 To make the eyeballs, squeeze an eyeball-size amount from one end of the white Half & Half, then roll it in your fingers to narrow the base. Pull it away from the rest of the Half & Half, and cut with a craft knife so that the eyeball "stem" is about 1 inch long. Repeat to make another 11 eyeballs.

6 Divide the brown Half & Half into 12 equal-size pieces, and roll each piece into a ball. Roll each ball into a sausage shape, flatten, and cut at an angle at one end to create an eyebrow shape. Attach to the cupcake above the eye socket with water.

7 To make the irises for the eyeballs, roll the blue Half & Half out very thinly on a counter dusted with cornstarch. Use the large end of a small plain piping tip to cut out 12 by ½-inch circles. Use water to attach one iris to each eyeball. Roll the black Half & Half out very thinly. Use the small end of the tip to cut out 12 pupils. Attach a pupil to the center of each iris with water.

8 Create the appearance of arteries on the eyeballs by drawing on branching lines with the red edible marker pen.

9 Fill the eye sockets with Piping Gel "Blood." Sink the "stem" of an eyeball into the gel in each cupcake and then use water to attach the eyeball to the edge of the cupcake, as if the eyeball has popped out of its socket.

know your zombie

In the *Wolfenstein* video games, what is the name of the player's character?

1. Edward Carnby

2. William "B.J." Blazkowicz

3. Chris Redfield

(The answer is on page 80.)

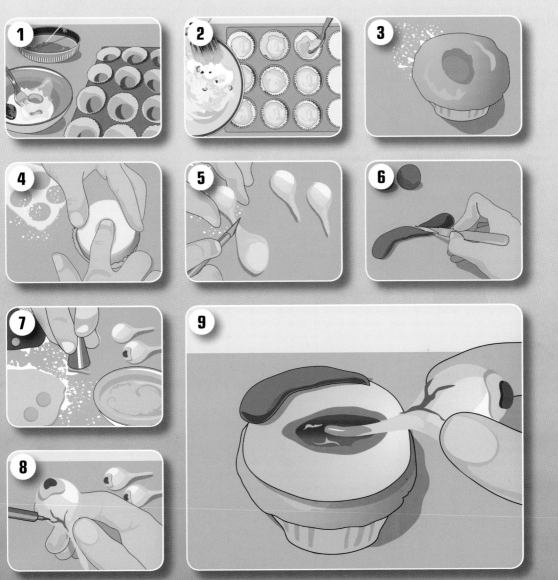

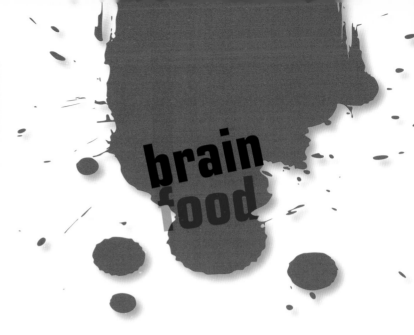

brain food

honey cupcakes

- ¼ cup honey
- ½ cup (4 oz/1 stick) unsalted butter
- ½ cup granulated sugar
- 1½ cups all-purpose, cake, or pastry flour
- 1½ tsp baking powder
- ½ tsp salt
- ½ tsp ground cinnamon
- ¼ tsp grated nutmeg
- 3 large eggs, beaten
- 5 tbsp milk

decorations

- 15 oz Half & Half, colored pink with 1 to 2 drops soft pink paste food coloring (see page 11)
- 3½ oz Royal Icing, colored peach with 2 drops peach paste food coloring (see page 10)
- ½ quantity Italian Meringue Buttercream (see page 9)
- cornstarch, for dusting
- 12 oz store-bought fondant, colored green with 1 drop green and a dab of red paste food coloring (see page 11)
- 4 oz clear piping gel

Brains are a delicacy in the cuisine of many cultures, and zombies are no exception. These sweet honey cupcakes with a delicious buttercream filling are the quintessential end to a big zombie meal. A useful survival tip you should know is that destroying a zombie's brain is a sure-fire way to kill it.

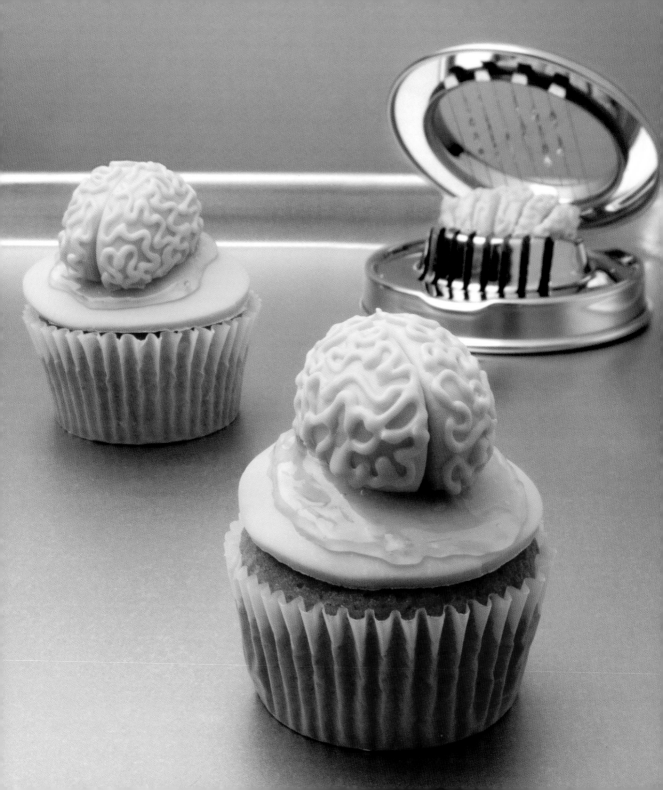

brain food

know your zombie

What was the budget for the video of Michael Jackson's 1983 song "Thriller?"

1. $100,000

2. $250,000

3. $500,000

(The answer is on page 80.)

1 Preheat the oven to 350°F. Line a 12-hole muffin pan with 12 paper cupcake liners. Put the honey, butter, and sugar in a large saucepan and heat gently, stirring constantly, until melted and combined. Pour the mixture into a large bowl and let cool.

2 Sift the flour, baking powder, salt, and spices into the honey mixture and stir together. Using an electric mixer, gradually beat in the eggs and then stir in the milk until smooth. Spoon the batter into the liners. Bake for about 25 minutes, turning once halfway through baking, until well risen and firm to the touch. Transfer to a wire rack and let cool.

3 To make the brains, divide the pink Half & Half into 12 equal-size pieces. Roll one piece into a ball and squeeze it gently from both sides to form an oval. Use the side of the end of a toothpick to score a groove down the center of the oval, creating the 2 hemispheres of the brain. Make sure that the groove curves all the way under the brain. Repeat to make another 11 brains.

4 Fit a pastry bag or parchment paper cone with a fine plain piping tip and fill with the peach Royal Icing. Put each brain on a square of acetate to hold it in place while you are piping, and pipe squiggles and curves all around one side of the brain. Repeat on the other side.

5 To fill the cupcakes, make a large hole in the center of each cupcake with the handle of a wooden spoon.

6 Fill a pastry bag with the Italian Meringue Buttercream and squeeze gently until the hole is filled and a small amount of buttercream comes out of the top.

7 Dust the counter with cornstarch and roll out the green fondant to a thickness of ⅛ inch. Using a 2½ to 3-inch round cutter, cut out 12 circles that will cover the cupcakes. Place a fondant circle on the top of each buttercream center.

8 Use a small amount of water to attach a brain to the center of each fondant circle. Fill a pastry bag or parchment paper cone fitted with a fine plain piping tip with the clear piping gel. Pipe the gel all around the base of each brain to make it look gooey.

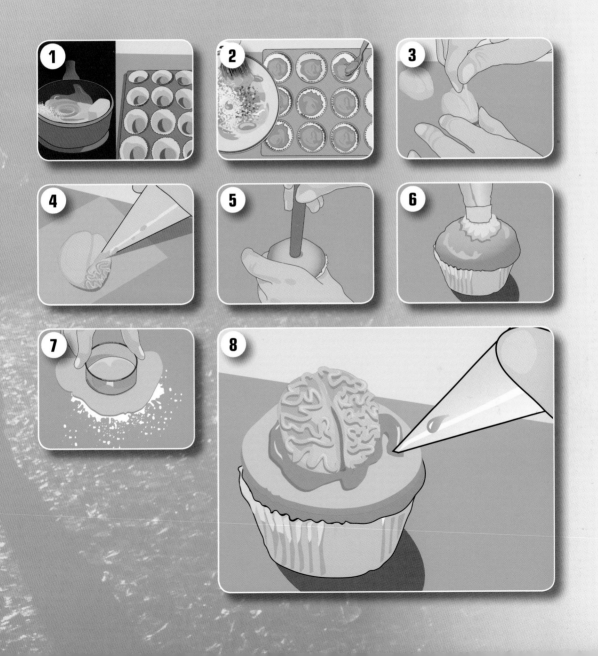

DIFFICULTY RATING

MAKES 12

Decorations can be made the same day as baking.

decapitated
zombie

gingerbread
cupcakes

- ¼ cup plus 2 tbsp milk
- ¾ tsp baking soda
- ½ cup plus 1 tbsp (4½ oz) unsalted butter, softened
- ½ cup firmly packed dark brown sugar
- ¼ cup blackstrap molasses
- 3 large eggs, beaten
- 1 cup plus 3 tbsp white all-purpose, cake, or pastry flour
- 1 tbsp ground ginger
- ¾ tsp ground cinnamon

decorations

- 12 large marshmallows
- 8 oz white couverture or baking chocolate
- 36 white hard mint candies (such as Tic Tacs)
- 6 oz Piping Gel "Blood" (see page 10)
- 8 oz Royal Icing, colored black with 18 drops black paste food coloring; or brown with 36 drops brown paste food coloring; or yellow with 4 drops yellow paste food coloring (see page 10)
- 12 Knives (see page 15; optional)

Imagine you are cornered by a zombie in your kitchen. If you have any hopes of surviving, your best bet is to grab the nearest butcher's knife and take a good swing. This heavenly gingerbread cupcake illustrates what a proud survivor might do after they've fought off the zombie's attack: display the severed head and brag. The head is made from a marshmallow dipped in melted white couverture—good-quality coating chocolate with a high percentage of cocoa butter.

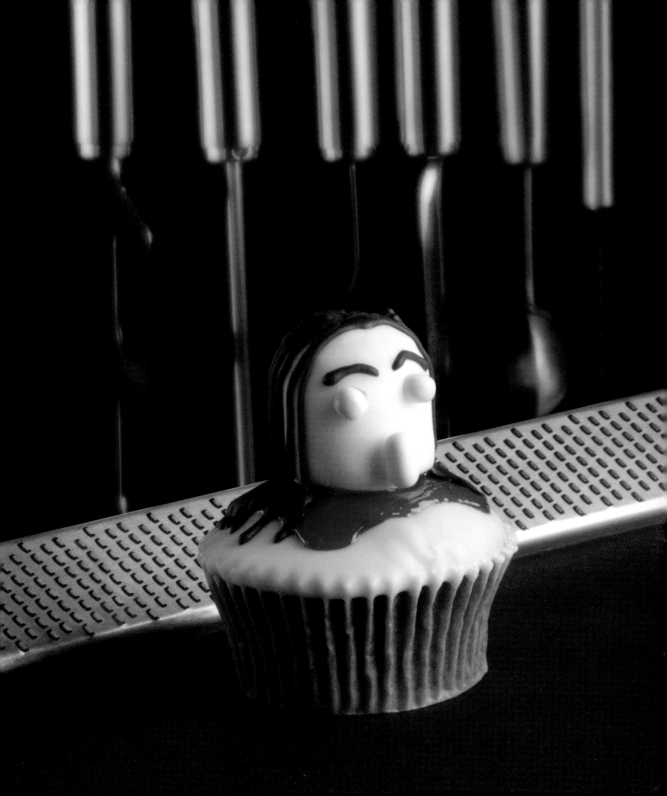

decapitated zombie

know your zombie

In Night of the Living Dead (1968), the hero Tom hacks up a zombie hand with a kitchen knife. What was this prop made from?

1. Clay filled with chocolate syrup

2. A rubber glove filled with tomato sauce

3. A medical prosthetic filled with real blood

(The answer is on page 80.)

1 Preheat the oven to 325°F. Line a 12-hole muffin pan with 12 paper cupcake liners. Put the milk in a bowl and stir in the baking soda until dissolved.

2 Put the butter and sugar in a large bowl and, using an electric mixer, beat together until pale and fluffy. Beat in the molasses and then gradually beat in the eggs. Sift the flour and spices into the mixture and beat together, then gradually beat in the milk mixture. Spoon the batter into the liners. Bake for about 25 minutes, turning once halfway through baking, until firm to the touch. Transfer to a wire rack and let cool.

3 For the heads, snip the corners off the top edge of each marshmallow using scissors and then cut into a domed shape. Insert a toothpick into the bottom of each marshmallow.

4 Melt the chocolate, stirring every 15 seconds, in a microwave oven on low or in a heatproof bowl set over a saucepan of gently simmering water. Dip the marshmallows into the melted chocolate up to the flat edge, allowing any extra chocolate to drip back into the bowl.

5 Stick a head-topped toothpick into each cooled cupcake so that it stands upright and let set. Meanwhile, put a small amount of chocolate on a mint candy and attach it to one head, just above the bottom edge, for a nose. Repeat for the other heads.

6 Use the tip of a craft knife to drill 2 eye sockets through the chocolate coating just above and on either side of the nose, making the holes slightly larger than the diameter of a mint candy. Press a mint candy into each eye socket. When set, remove the head-topped toothpicks from the cupcakes. Remelt the leftover chocolate, dip the top of each cupcake into the chocolate, and let set.

7 When set, fill a pastry bag or parchment paper cone fitted with a fine plain piping tip with Piping Gel "Blood" and pipe a pool of dripping blood on each cupcake, for the severed head to sit on. Remove the heads from the toothpicks and then place them in the blood.

8 Use black, brown, or yellow Royal Icing in a pastry bag or parchment paper cone fitted with a fine plain piping tip to pipe eyebrows and hair on the decapitated head. If desired, smear a Knife with Piping Gel "Blood" and attach to each cupcake in front of the severed head.

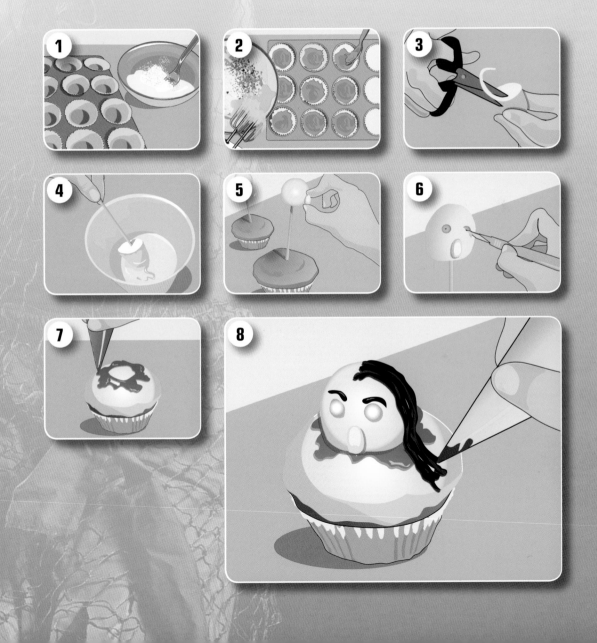

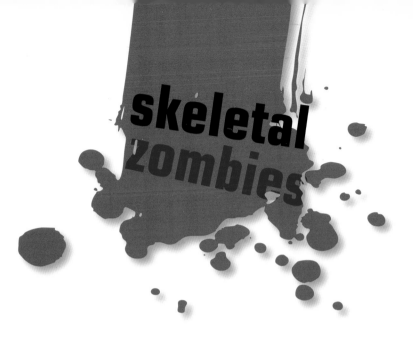

DIFFICULTY RATING

MAKES **12**

Make the decorations the day
before baking.

chocolate-mint
cupcakes

- ½ cup (4 oz/1 stick) unsalted butter, softened
- 1 cup granulated sugar
- 3 large eggs, beaten
- ⅔ cup milk
- 1 tsp mint extract
- 1⅓ cups all-purpose, cake, or pastry flour
- ¼ cup unsweetened cocoa
- 1½ tsp baking powder
- ¼ tsp salt
- ½ cup mini semisweet chocolate chips

decorations

- 6 oz plain white Half & Half (see page 11)
- plain vegetable shortening, for greasing
- about 120 white hard mint candies
  (such as Tic Tacs)
- 1 quantity Dark Chocolate Ganache
  (see page 8)
- edible black marker pen (optional)
- 12 Knives (see page 15)
- ¾ oz Piping Gel "Blood" (see page 10)

Since zombies are already undead, killing them again isn't easy.
One of the less well-known techniques for surviving a zombie
attack is to sever your zombie assailant's spinal cord. This minty,
chocolaty delight gives you pointers on where exactly to insert
the knife. Each cupcake is topped by a generous swirl of
chocolate ganache. The head is attached to the cupcake with
a toothpick, so be sure to warn your guests to remove the
toothpick before they take a bite.

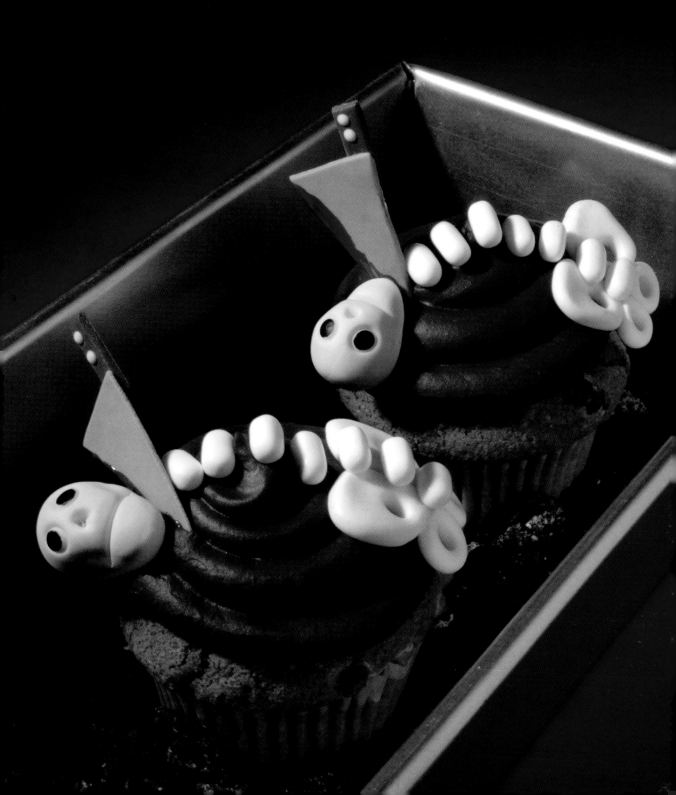

skeletal zombies

1 The day before, make the decorations. Using 3 oz of the Half & Half, roll two ¼-inch balls and two ½-inch balls for each cupcake, to create the pelvis (you will have some Half & Half left over for the skulls). Roll out the larger balls into ovals and press them flat on to two strips of acetate, each 4 by 11 inches (see page 11). Using a paintbrush, paint the facing edges of the 2 flat ovals with water and press together so that they are attached and the ovals narrow at the bottom.

2 Paint the bottoms of the ovals with water. Press the 2 small balls flat below the joined ovals to form the bottom of the pelvic bone. The frosting shape should resemble a butterfly at this stage.

3 Paint water in the center of the pelvic bone, and press on 2 to 3 mint candies, side by side, to create the base of the spinal column. Using the small end of a medium plain piping tip, cut 4 holes from the pelvic bone. Repeat to make another 11 pelvic bones.

4 To make the skulls, roll 12 ovals from the remaining Half & Half. Use a craft knife to cut partway into each oval, about a third of the way up, to create the mouth. Use the piping tip again to indent circles for eyes. With the blunt end of a toothpick, make an indentation below the eyes to create the nose. If desired, use the black edible marker pen to paint in the eyes. Gently push a toothpick into the base of each skull and let the decorations dry, uncovered, overnight.

5 Preheat the oven to 350°F. Line a 12-hole muffin pan with 12 paper cupcake liners. Put the butter and sugar in a large bowl and, using an electric mixer, beat together until pale and fluffy. Gradually beat in the eggs and then stir in the milk and mint extract.

6 Sift the flour, cocoa, baking powder, and salt into the mixture and then fold in using a large wooden spoon. Spoon the batter into the paper cases. Sprinkle the chocolate chips over the tops of the cupcakes. Bake for about 25 minutes, turning once halfway through baking, until well risen and firm to the touch. Transfer to a wire rack and let cool.

7 When the cupcakes are cool, pipe a round swirl of Dark Chocolate Ganache on the top of each. Press the pelvis on one side of the cupcake, and use 6 to 7 mint candies, placed side by side, to create a spinal cord.

8 Place the tip of a Knife into the ganache at the place where the mint candies end on each cupcake. Use Piping Gel "Blood" in a pastry bag or parchment paper cone fitted with a fine plain piping tip to add some gore.

9 Use a toothpick to hold the severed skull to the side of each cupcake about ½ inch away from the spinal cord, to make it look as if it has dropped off.

know your zombie

In whose mansion does the group take refuge in the movie *Zombieland* (2009)?

1. **Bill Murray's**

2. **Dan Aykroyd's**

3. **Harold Ramis's**

(The answer is on page 80.)

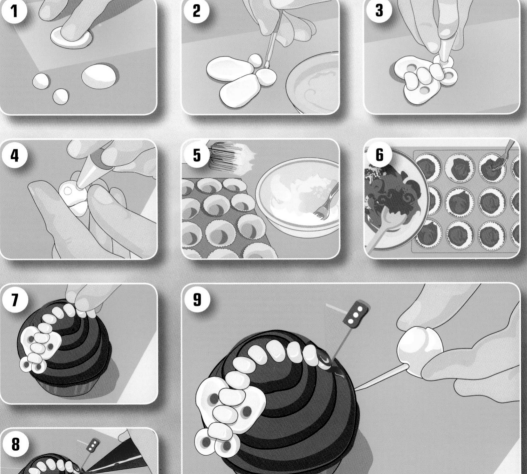
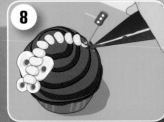

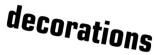

bludgeon to survive

DIFFICULTY RATING

MAKES 12

Make the decorations the day before baking.

pumpkin cupcakes

- ⅔ cup vegetable oil
- 4 large eggs
- ¾ cup plus 2 tbsp granulated sugar
- 7 oz (about ¾ cup) canned pumpkin
- 1½ cups all-purpose, cake, or pastry flour
- ½ tsp baking powder
- ¼ tsp baking soda
- ¼ tsp ground cloves
- ¼ tsp grated nutmeg
- ¾ tsp ground cinnamon
- ¼ tsp salt

In many zombie movies, the heroes have to survive using whatever improvised instrument they can lay their hands on. These cupcakes are a little battered from the crowbar, shovel, and baseball bat decorations, but, just like you after you've tasted them, they just keep on coming back for more.

decorations

- 4 Baseball Bats (see page 15)
- 4 Shovels (see page 15)
- 4 Crowbars (see page 15)
- cornstarch, for dusting
- ¾ oz Half & Half, colored black with 2 drops black paste food coloring (see page 11)
- ¾ oz plain white Half & Half
- red edible marker pen
- 1¾ oz Royal Icing, colored black with 4 drops black paste food coloring (see page 10)
- 1¾ oz plain white Royal Icing

vanilla cream glaze

- 1¾ cups confectioners' sugar
- ¼ cup heavy whipping cream
- 2 tsp pure vanilla extract
- ¼ tsp salt
- 2 drops green paste food coloring
- 1 drop yellow paste food coloring
- 3 drops purple paste food coloring

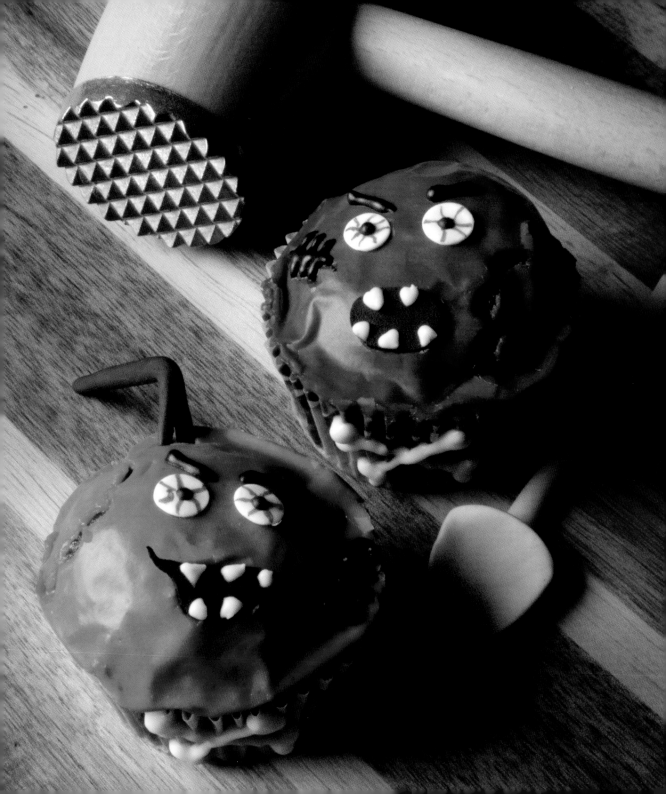

bludgeon to survive

know your zombie

In the video game *Left 4 Dead 2* (2009), which of these items cannot be used by the players to bludgeon the zombies?

1. Baseball bat

2. Crowbar

3. Shovel

(The answer is on page 80.)

1 The day before, make your weapons —Crowbars, Shovels, and Baseball Bats—and let dry, uncovered, overnight (see page 15). The following day, make the cupcakes. Preheat the oven to 325°F. Line a 12-hole muffin pan with 12 paper cupcake liners. Put the oil, eggs, sugar, and pumpkin in a large bowl and, using an electric mixer, beat together until combined and smooth.

2 Sift in the flour, baking powder, baking soda, spices, and salt and mix together. Spoon the batter into the liners. Bake for about 25 minutes, turning once halfway through baking, until well risen and firm to the touch. Transfer to a wire rack and let cool.

3 When the cupcakes are cool, make the Vanilla Cream Glaze. Put the confectioners' sugar, heavy cream, vanilla extract, and salt in a medium bowl and mix together with a wooden spoon until smooth. Transfer half the mixture to another bowl. Add the green and yellow food colorings to one bowl to color bright green, and purple food coloring to the other bowl to color bright purple. Dip 6 cupcakes into the green glaze and the remaining cupcakes into the purple glaze.

4 Press the small end of a medium plain piping tip into the glaze repeatedly in a curved shape to make the appearance of a bite mark. Let the glaze set for 20 minutes.

5 Dust the counter with cornstarch. Roll the black Half & Half into a ball and then roll out the ball very thinly. Use a craft knife to cut out 12 mouth shapes.

6 Roll the white Half & Half into a ball and roll out very thinly. Use the piping tip again to cut out 24 small circles for eyes.

7 Use the red edible marker pen to add veins to the eyes. Fill a pastry bag or parchment paper cone fitted with a fine plain piping tip with the black Royal Icing and pipe an eyeball in the center of each eye.

8 Use a small amount of white Royal Icing to attach 2 eyes and a mouth to each cupcake. Use the black Royal Icing to pipe suture lines on one side of the face and to give the zombies mean eyebrows.

9 Fill a pastry bag or parchment paper cone fitted with a fine plain piping tip with the white Royal Icing and use to pipe teeth in the mouths and crossbones on the cupcake liners.

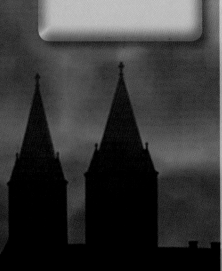

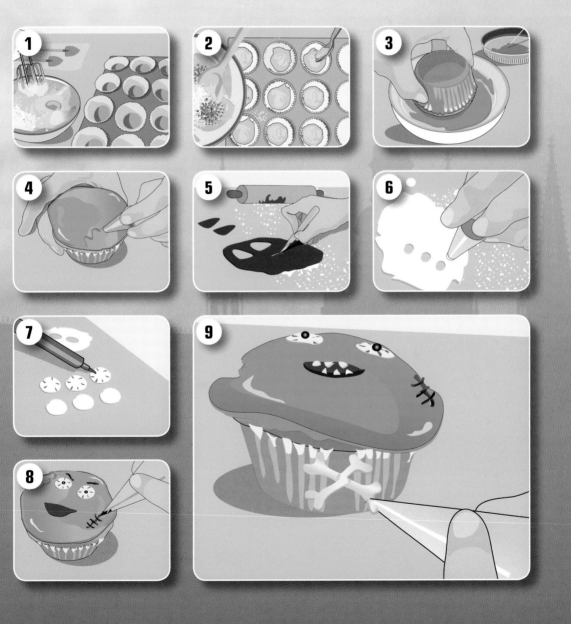

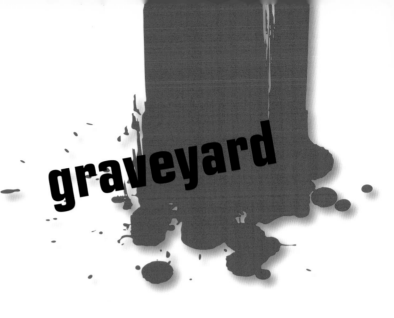

graveyard

DIFFICULTY RATING

MAKES **12**

Make the decorations the day before baking.

fudge brownie
cupcakes

- 8 oz semisweet baking chocolate
- 6 tbsp unsalted butter
- 1 cup granulated sugar
- 3 large eggs
- ¾ cup all-purpose, cake, or pastry flour
- ¼ cup unsweetened cocoa
- pinch of baking soda
- ¼ tsp salt
- ¾ cup chopped walnuts

decorations

- 4 Gravestones (see page 13)
- 1 Cross (see page 13)
- 3 oz Half & Half, colored black with 5 to 8 drops black paste food coloring (see page 11)
- ½ quantity Dark Chocolate Ganache (see page 8)
- 2 Rats (see page 14)
- 1½ cups finely crushed chocolate cookie crumbs
- 1 Shovel (see page 15; optional)

Beady-eyed rats, fallen crosses, and broken gravestones adorn any respectable graveyard. Those who are familiar with zombies know that just because they are buried doesn't mean they will stay buried. These brownie cupcakes create an entire graveyard when arranged together. Add a Shovel filled with cookie crumb earth to make it look like you are still digging a grave.

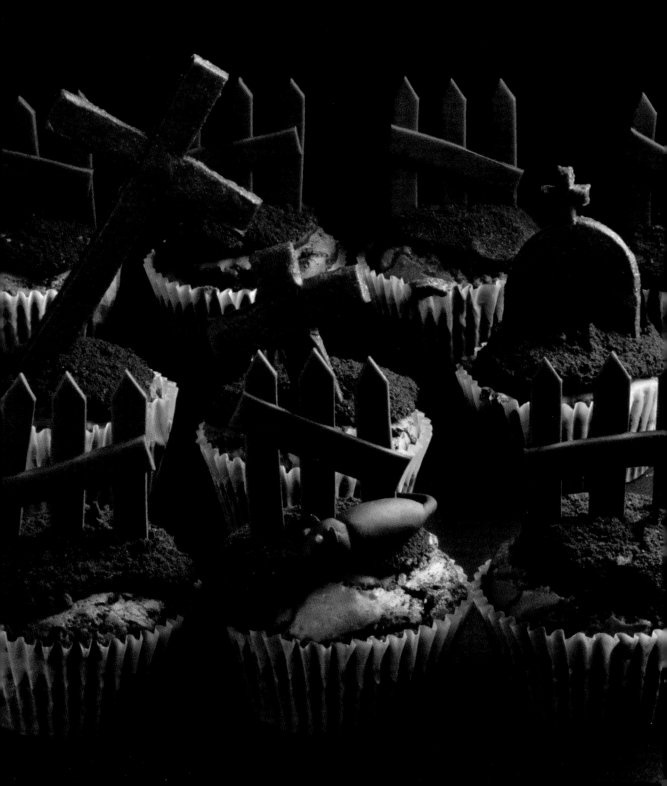

graveyard

1 The day before, make the Gravestones and Cross decorations. Also make the fences the day before so that they can dry. Roll out the Half & Half to make the cupcake toppers using a strip of acetate 3 by 10 inches (see page 11).

2 Using a craft knife, cut the Half & Half into a strip measuring 1¾ by 8 inches. Make vertical cuts at ⅜-inch intervals along the entire length. You will need 16 strips in total.

3 To create a fence section, place 3 black strips, ¼ inch apart, on a clean piece of acetate. Cut off the top 2 corners of each strip to create a point.

4 Use a small amount of water to attach a fourth strip at an angle across the 3 pointed fence pickets. Repeat with the remaining strips to make 4 fence sections. Let dry, uncovered, overnight.

5 Preheat the oven to 350°F. Line a 12-hole muffin pan with 12 paper cupcake liners. Break the chocolate into a heatproof bowl set over a saucepan of gently simmering water. Add the butter and heat gently, stirring constantly, until melted and combined. Remove from the heat and let cool.

6 Put the sugar and eggs in a large bowl and, using an electric mixer, beat together. Sift in the flour, cocoa, baking soda, and salt and mix together. Add the chocolate mixture and walnuts and stir together. Spoon the batter into the liners. Bake for about 30 minutes, turning once halfway through baking, until the tops are set, but the centers are still slightly moist. Transfer to a wire rack and let cool.

7 To assemble the graveyard, pipe a swirl of Dark Chocolate Ganache onto each cupcake, leaving some of the cupcake showing. Arrange the cupcakes in 3 rows of 4. Place a section of fence on each of the cupcakes in the front row.

8 Prop the Gravestones on random cupcakes in the back and middle rows at angles; you can break a Gravestone cookie and prop it in pieces so that it appears even more decrepit. Place the Rats so that they appear to scurry around the Gravestones and fence. Cut a slit in one of the cupcakes on the back row and carefully push the Cross into it, leaning it at a slight angle.

9 To complete the scene, sprinkle chocolate cookie crumbs around the graveyard to resemble earth. A Shovel also looks great stuck in a cupcake, with extra cookie crumbs, as if it's digging a fresh grave.

know your zombie

Whose grave were the bickering siblings Barbra and Johnny going to visit in the beginning of *Night of the Living Dead* (1968)?

1. Their father's
2. Their mother's
3. Their dog's

(The answer is on page 80.)

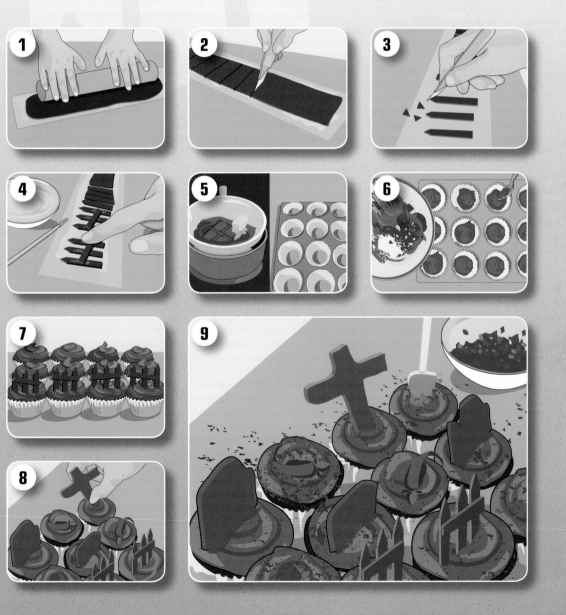

index

trivia answers

p18: 2. Infected lab chimpanzees
p22: 3. The Hive
p26: 1. Wade Davis
p30: 1. The zombies start to die of starvation
p34: 1. *Jane Eyre*
p38: 2. Zack Snyder
p42: 2. The Winchester
p46: 1. "I kick ass for the Lord!"

p50: 3. *Pride and Prejudice*
p58: 2. William "B.J." Blazkowicz
p62: 3. $500,000
p66: 1. Clay filled with chocolate syrup
p70: 1. Bill Murray's
p74: 3. Shovel
p78: 1. Their father's

Acknowledgments

Kitchen equipment supplied by
Premier Gourmet
3465 Delaware Ave
Buffalo, NY 14217
www.premiergourmet.com

Gourmet facilities for the photoshoot were provided by
Artisan Kitchens and Baths
200 Amherst Street
Buffalo, NY 14207
www.artisankitchensandbaths.com